TURN YOUR
SETBACKS INTO
COMEBACKS

TURN YOUR SETBACKS INTO COMEBACKS

RICK McDANIEL

CROSSLINK
PUBLISHING

I often tell people that it's far easier to fall down than to get up. Rick McDaniel has written a great book on that subject – how to turn setbacks into comebacks. It's a good read and you will be enriched!

Dr. George O. Wood
General Superintendent
The Assemblies of God

In his new book Rick McDaniel doesn't only teach the techniques of turning things around, he shows the importance of a right heart behind it. No matter where you find yourself in life, you will experience setbacks. Allow Rick to give you the tools needed to turn them into comebacks.

Rob Ketterling
Lead Pastor | River Valley Church | Author

Rick McDaniel understands what it takes to have a comeback. In this amazing new book he helps us find the right skills, tools and attitude to turn our lives around. His practical advice will help you get ready for your comeback.

Tim Storey
Author/Speaker/Life Coach

Rick McDaniel is a great writer who has written a powerful book. This book has encouraged me to pull myself together, gather my strength and continue to pursue my calling. Prepare to be strengthened and encouraged.

Harry R. Jackson Jr.
Bishop, International Communion of Evangelical Churches

DEDICATION

To Tim Storey:
You have been a great friend to me for over thirty years
and you've helped so many people believe comebacks
are possible.

ACKNOWLEDGEMENTS

There are always many people to thank whenever a big project is accomplished.

The staff of Richmond Community Church does so much to allow me the opportunity to write and impact lives.

My assistant, Terri Connell, has helped in many ways with this book.

David Daniels provided a place to write in a moment of urgency.

Lucas and Liz Munn let me use their beach house on multiple occasions in order to get this book finished.

Rick Bates and the staff of CrossLink have made this book a reality.

And my wife, Michelle, who is a source of constant support.

TABLE OF CONTENTS

INTRODUCTION

Comebacks are possible—they happen all the time. But if you have had a setback, a comeback may seem impossible to you. This book is about how to make a personal comeback, and that it can begin for you today. You can have a comeback from career setbacks, relational setbacks, financial setbacks, health setbacks, and even spiritual setbacks. If you are willing to put into practice the principles in this book you will move past any setback in your life. You can have an incredible comeback!

Apple is one of the most profitable and highly regarded companies in the world. It is hard to imagine a company that is doing better or has a brighter future than Apple. Their brand loyalty is the envy of every business. The 2001 release of the iPod has changed how people listen to music, the 2007 release of the iPhone has changed how people use cellular phones, the 2010 release of the iPad has changed how people use all forms of media, and the 2014 release of the iWatch is bringing the next huge change in personal communication. These impressive products sell at phenomenal rates, and this is on top of their line of personal computers that have a very large customer base.

Yet, in 1997 Apple was on the verge of bankruptcy. As hard as it is to believe today, Apple was in desperate need of a comeback. Steve Jobs returned to lead the company and moved them from their setback to make a comeback.

Our entire country experienced a huge economic setback in 2008 with the Great Recession. The impact of what happened is unprecedented in our generation. Declines in consumer spending, which occurred in 2008 and 2009, were the first consecutive declines since the 1930s. Since World War II, annual consumption spending had only fallen twice before—in 1974 and 1980. Unemployment was at levels that had not been seen in over a generation. We needed a massive financial comeback.

But we have made a comeback. Unemployment rates are back to prerecession levels. The entire automotive industry has had an incredible comeback. Not long ago the government literally had to bail out the industry, yet this year sales are at an all-time high. If the projections are correct, sales for 2015 will be 17.8 million vehicles, breaking the annual record. The housing industry is also having a comeback. Home sales are the best since February 2007. They are on track to rise this year to their highest level in many years. Wages need to increase and more high-paying jobs need to be created, but we are moving past the setback and into the comeback.

I live in Richmond, VA, and we had a front-row seat to one of the best comebacks in recent memory. Virginia Commonwealth University had ended their 2011 college basketball season poorly. The team lost five of their last eight games and finished fourth in the Colonial Athletic Association. They did do well in the Conference tournament, but lost in the championship game. The program had success in recent years and this was certainly a setback year. They did not have high hopes for making the NCAA tournament, not even gathering together as a team on Selection Sunday. But they were selected amidst much controversy, having to play in one of the newly created play-in games. The VCU basketball team decided a comeback was in order. They reeled off five straight wins in the tournament against highly ranked teams, including the number one seed, Kansas, and ended up making the Final Four. VCU had never made the Final Four and, considering the ending to their season, this was a comeback for the ages (at least in Richmond).

An individual comeback is what this book is ultimately about. The Minnesota Vikings running back Adrian Peterson tore his ACL Christmas Eve in 2012, but the next season was his greatest year as a pro football player. After a surgery that turns dominant players into ordinary ones, Peterson rushed for 2097 yards, just eight shy of the all-time NFL rushing record. NFL quarterback Peyton Manning had four neck surgeries and some thought he would never play football again; few thought he would return to his QB All-Pro status. After missing an entire season, his team the Indianapolis Colts let him go, and the Denver Broncos signed him hoping he could return to his MVP form. Return he did, being named to the Pro Bowl and helping his team to win the Super Bowl.

Even the great Tiger Woods needed a comeback. His setbacks have been well-documented: marital infidelity followed by divorce, three years without winning a PGA tournament and multiple injuries. After all those setbacks anyone, even Tiger Woods, needed a comeback. His comeback started in early 2013 when he shot his lowest score ever in a final round at the Honda Classic and went on to win the Arnold Palmer at Bay Hill. He then won again at the Memorial Tournament in spectacular fashion. He won the "fifth major"—the Players Championship—and won another World Golf Championship at the Bridgestone Invitational. His five wins made him number one in FedEx points for the season, the number one-ranked golfer in the world, and the Player of the Year on the PGA tour. Quite a comeback but now, thanks to another surgery, he is again in need of a comeback. He has to rehab his injuries and work to recapture his dominant game.

The question is not will there be comebacks, but will one of those comebacks be yours. Just as setbacks come in all shapes and sizes, so do comebacks. But there are certain principles that govern comebacks. Putting into practice these principles will help you move past your setback. Everyone—from athletes, to celebrities, to industries—has proven it is possible. You have the potential to write your comeback story. So comebacks are possible, in fact even probable, knowing and applying the right information. If you are ready for your comeback—let's go!

BELIEVING IN YOUR COMEBACK

In the Gospels, the first four books of the New Testament—Matthew, Mark, Luke, and John—tell the story of the life of Jesus. 125 times Jesus makes an imperative statement like "Love others," for instance. He says 125 of them and they are on a number of different topics or themes. Of those 125, the number one theme that he touches on, twenty-one times, the next one is eight times, is a variation of this: "Don't be afraid," "Fear not," "Have courage." The eight, by the way, is the "Love Others" theme. What makes Christianity unique is we are the faith that teaches love. Yet, even though love is the central theme of Christianity, the number one statement that Jesus makes more than any other statement is "Don't be fearful. Don't be afraid. Be courageous. Have courage."

The apostle Paul puts it this way in II Timothy 1:7: "God's Spirit doesn't make cowards out of us. The Spirit gives us power, love, and self-control." If you're going to have a comeback, you must believe you can. You must overcome your fear of the future. The Spirit doesn't make cowards out of us. God doesn't want us to live in fear. God wants to deliver us from our fears and launch us into a marvelous comeback.

CNN and **USA Today** asked the Gallup organization to do a poll in 1998. The question was, "What do you believe will happen by the year 2025?" Forty-nine percent thought there would be a worldwide collapse of the economy. I think the worldwide recession that began in 2008 could apply. Sixty-six percent of people said an environmental catastrophe. There have been some environmental disasters like the Gulf Oil Spill, but maybe not a catastrophe. Seventy-six percent thought there would be the emergence of a deadly new disease. Ebola might suffice, but maybe not. Forty-eight percent said there would be a military strike or attack using nuclear weapons. The aggression of Russia and the fanaticism of Iran make this a future possibility.

Resist Being Fear Filled

Some bad things have happened and some bad things haven't. There are certainly plenty of things you could be fearful about, but you need to resist being fear-filled. Resist it. Fear breeds fear. The more we focus on it, the more exaggerated and distorted it becomes. The worst thing you can do to your comeback is to be fear-focused. If you allow your life to be filled with fear, it will breed upon itself, expanding and reproducing even more fear.

Fear creates spiritual amnesia, and we forget all the good things God has done. We seem to forget all the ways God has carried us through various situations. We get so focused on the setback we have amnesia about the fact God has brought us through time and time again. I think about my own life and how God has provided and taken care of me, yet fear can get a hold of us and we forget how good God is.

Fear also turns us into control freaks. A setback leaves us with such a sense of loss of control we end up wanting to control even more whatever we can control. This is very negative in many aspects of our lives. It's a negative from a relational standpoint. It's a negative from a spiritual standpoint. You can try to do everything yourself as if God isn't even real and doesn't even work in your life. You try to control things because you feel that so many things are out of control. You can't believe in your comeback and be a control freak.

Another negative as fear takes hold of our lives is it makes security our god. Now our true god is security and safety. What we seek out is the safest thing, the safest place, the most secure feeling. But God never placed you on this earth to be safe. He placed you on this earth for a great adventure of how He is going to work in your life. And you will miss out on so much that God has for you if you try to build these safety walls or you try to hunker down into your bunker and make everything safe. You cannot create security and safety for yourself as hard as you may try.

Thirty years ago, the most popular dog in America was the poodle. It was so popular especially compared to the Rottweiler there were less than 1,000 Rottweilers in the entire country. Today the number of poodles has plummeted. There are half as many poodles as there used to be, but there are 100 times more Rottweilers than there used to be. Nobody has ever been scared of a miniature poodle, but people are certainly scared of Rottweilers. It tells you something about fear and our desire for security.

And while you focus on security and safety, opportunities pass you by. Good things don't even get noticed. You miss your comeback! If you give into fear, you will miss out. You will miss out on the good things that God has for you. You won't even be able to see your comeback because your sole focus will be safety and security. Resist the fear.

Fear corrodes our confidence in the goodness of God. Either God is good or He isn't. If He is good, then you don't need to be afraid. Fear is *False Evidence Appearing Real.*

Don't allow it to get a hold of your life. Fight against it. You have to resist fear and you have to choose faith over fear. That is a choice. You choose faith. You choose to trust. We must choose to have faith and not to give into fear.

Choose Faith Over Fear

I couldn't help but chuckle when I was looking at the **MSN Money** website one week and the big headline was, "Your Biggest Enemy Now? Fear." Some people are losing thousands, tens of thousands, and hundreds of thousands of dollars because of fear. They are making fear-based decisions instead of faith-based decisions. I am a believer in faith-based decision-making, not fear-based decision-making. You overcome your setback and move into your comeback by making faith-based decisions.

You choose faith over fear. You choose faith. If you will exercise greater and greater faith, you will automatically diminish fear. It's like a mathematical formula. The more faith that you exercise, the less fear you will have— guaranteed. More faith, less fear; they move in direct proportion to each other. The higher the faith goes, the lower the fear goes.

If you discipline your thinking and replace fearful thoughts with faith-filled thoughts, you will move yourself right into your comeback. When God's Spirit is in us, we don't have to be afraid. God's Spirit gives us power, love, and self-control. The Spirit gives us what we need to move past our setbacks and into a comeback.

Fear is limiting. Fear is draining. Fear is contagious. You cannot allow fear to limit your potential, to restrain what you can do with your life or cap your comeback. You can't let it deplete you of all your courage. Joshua 1:9 says, "I've commanded you to be strong and brave. Don't ever been afraid or discouraged. I am the Lord your God and I will be there to help you wherever you go."

Fear is contagious, and it is amazing how it can spread. Before you know it, people, families, teams, companies, departments can't move forward. They won't try. They won't step out. They won't innovate. They won't create. What if it doesn't work? What if it's a failure?

Fear of Failure

Fear of failure holds you back. And God doesn't want you to be afraid to fail. Remember: everyone will fail. Everyone. No one has ever had a comeback without some failures along the way. Ecclesiastes 7: 20 says: "No one in this world always does right." This is the Bible's wisdom: no one ever goes through life without failures. No one always does right. No one bats a thousand. In baseball, if you bat .300 you are a star, though it means you didn't succeed seven of ten times. Isn't that funny? In baseball you can succeed three out of ten times and they call you an all-star. If you succeed three out of ten times in life, you're considered yourself a failure. Everyone will fail. No one is perfect. Warren Buffett loses money, LeBron James misses free throws, and Lincoln made bad decisions. Even the great ones make mistakes.

The fear of failure comes from unrealistic expectations. On the door of the training facility of the New England Patriots, one of the most successful professional football franchises, it says: "Manage Your Expectations." You can't win every game. You shouldn't expect everything will always work out. You will fail, and you need to deal with it. Better to remember everyone fails.

The fear of failure can be more damaging than failure itself, because the fear of failure keeps you from ever trying when some things might have worked. So the fear of failure is worse than failure. Fear of failure is keeping you from your comeback. You need to compartmentalize your life so you'll have less fear of failure. There are many aspects of any person's life. There is your personal health. There are your personal relationships. There is your professional life. There is your mental health. There is your spiritual life. And if you fail in one of those areas, it doesn't mean you are a failure. You can't let the fear of failing keep you from pursuing your comeback, keep you from being courageous and bold.

Fear of failure causes indecisiveness so you are not able to act, especially as it relates to opportunities. God presents an opportunity before us, but fear of failure will cause us to hesitate, will cause us to be indecisive so we do not act. There is a window of opportunity and it opens and it closes. And when it closes it's gone. Fear of failure creates perfectionism. There is a difference between excellence and perfectionism. Excellence is a standard that you pursue. Perfectionism is a drive you can't be free of and you're never at peace. Everything can't always be perfect, and fear of failure will drive a person to have perfectionist tendencies. You need to be free of the fear of failure. And the way to be free of it is to understand if you fail you are in a very large club called the human race.

Napoleon was the second lowest in his entire class in his academic performance and he became, at one time, the most powerful man in the entire world. H.R. Macy founded Macy's department store. Seven times he failed at business, but he kept coming back and his namesake is on Macy's stores all around this country. I have great admiration for Abraham Lincoln and respect his leadership, but the man failed incredibly. He failed in relationships. He failed in business. He failed in politics. He failed far more times than he ever succeeded. He is an incredible comeback story. His greatest success was saving the United States of America. He is the greatest president of the greatest country the world has ever known. His leadership principles live on to this day and inspire me and many other leaders.

Failure Is Not Final

Psychologists have a phrase they call *awfulizing*. Awfulizing is when we inflate a failure to ridiculous proportions, making it so awful, so terrible. We blow it up. And it keeps us from moving forward pursuing and taking risks. What is life if you don't try new things and take risks? It is called a boring life. Jesus doesn't want you to just exist, He wants you to thrive. To do it, you've got to step out of your comfort zone. Failure is not reaching your goal. It's not setting a goal. Failure is not fulfilling your dream. It's not having a dream. Failure is not having a setback. It's refusing to attempt a comeback. Failure isn't final.

Half of all churches that are started never make it. Does that mean we should stop planting churches and new multi sites? I hope not. People can't experience Jesus in a way that they can relate to and understand because we might fail? Three quarters of all restaurants fail. We shouldn't start any new restaurants and just stick with what we have? Some people are successful with one restaurant concept and not with another. Failure is final only when we become negative—when we say things like "God is against me," or "I'm never going to get married," or "I'll never have financial security." Failure only becomes final when we become negative and quit trying, when we are not brave and courageous. We keep trying, we keep risking, and we keep advancing. Failure actually has benefits.

Failure Has Benefits

One of the benefits of failure or a setback is it shows we are functioning outside of our giftedness, meaning no one can be good at everything. You have to know what you are good at, what you are gifted for, and what it is God wants you to do. One of the things I have always resisted is when people try to get me to do what they think a pastor should do. God has given me certain gifts that if I use them will make me successful, but if I get out of my giftedness, it's not pretty and it doesn't work out very well. If you've had a setback, God may be saying to you, "Stay in your giftedness. Use the talents and gifts I have given you and don't get off in other areas that you are not gifted in and that I never gave you talents for."

Failure shows us what doesn't work; it is a marvelous educator. The great thing about failure is it teaches us, "Don't do that again." What is the definition of insanity? Doing the same thing the same way and expecting different results. Failure coaches us to do it a different way. Sometimes we just need to fine-tune or correct a little bit to be successful. Sometimes the idea is good but the timing is off. The timing causes it to fail. You have to line up the idea with timing that makes it successful. Failure shows us what doesn't work and forces us to find new approaches. Failure can be motivational; it motivates us to try something else. This is exactly what happened in the life of Abraham Lincoln. All of his failures motivated him to be exceptionally successful in his greatest challenge. He used the failures as motivation and it worked.

Failure has a marvelous way of preventing arrogance and pride because failure is very humbling. So just when you think you've arrived, just when you think you've made it, good old failure will bring you back to reality. I've had a little experience in this. You have a lot of success and you can think every idea is the greatest idea in the world. Then you fail, you have a setback, and it brings a necessary and appropriate humility. It shouldn't stop you from trying, but it does bring a degree of humility into your life that is very beneficial. The blessing of failure is it causes us to evaluate our lives. It opens us up to new directions. There is nothing like a setback to cause you to reflect, to cause you to be introspective. So failure has benefits, and those benefits can help you to make a comeback.

Fear Robs Us

Fear keeps us from loving deeply, keeps us from giving freely, and keeps us from dreaming wildly. It keeps you from loving deeply because when you are afraid you don't want to risk, and only in risk can you experience satisfying relationships. Do you really want to keep everything on the surface? You need to go deep. When you never go deep, you can never know the kind of true and loving relationships worth investing in.

Fear keeps us from giving freely because if you've got a scarcity mentality, you think there is only so much. You can't part with the little bit you have and then you are never able to give freely. And without giving freely, you cannot be blessed. It's more blessed to give than to receive. It's only when we give that we are able to receive. We have to sow in order to reap: no sowing, no reaping.

Fear keeps us from dreaming wildly because you can't have wild, crazy dreams if you are filled with fear. So the idea of taking risks is abhorrent to you. You play it safe and miss out. Whatever life is like without dreams I don't want to know. I don't want to live like that one day of my life. If I wake up a day of my life and I don't have dreams, I don't want to live. You can't believe in your comeback if you don't have dreams.

But you can choose faith over fear. You know what else you can do? You can ask God to have more faith. That's what Thomas did. Thomas said to Jesus, "Help my unbelief." He said, "Jesus, I want to believe, but you coming back from the dead, it's just kind of incredible!" Jesus said to him, "Do you see where the nail went through my hand?" Jesus walked right through a wall. He was on this side and came out on that side. Thomas witnessed it but he still said, "Help my unbelief."

Ask for Greater Faith

Maybe this is where you are. Maybe that is the level of your faith right now. You have had a setback, and your ability to believe a comeback is possible is very low. Just ask God to help you have greater faith and he will. God will help you. You may wonder how he does that: He does it in many ways, but I'll tell you one way He does it—He helps us to see things that have been there but we just haven't noticed. He helps us see things and the more we see things, we start thinking about coincidences. We think this is interesting or that was kind of lucky. And when you find yourself thinking all those things, then the light goes on. God is working, God does orchestrate events, and maybe I should just trust him more. You see it and the more you see it, the more you can believe.

You have to trust God's future plan for your life. God has a plan. It's a plan that involves your future, and you need to trust it. You don't need to fear the future if you know God has a plan. If you know God doesn't have a plan, you should start being very fearful. But God has a plan, and part of that plan involves your comeback.

It's like the soldier that gets captured and taken away to another country. He is all by himself and he doesn't know anything about what is going on with his family or his homeland. But then in the middle of his imprisonment, he gets a letter from his family and it says, "We're waiting for you to come home. Everything is fine here. Don't worry."

Now not one thing has changed about that soldier's situation. He is still in prison, still a prisoner of war, still suffering terribly at the hands of his captors. But his whole outlook changes because he knows everything is fine at home. He thinks, *Someday I'll be going home and people are waiting for me.* If God has a plan and He does, nothing takes God by surprise. So we trust God's plan. And you can know God's plan; when you know God's plan, you can move confidently into your future. You don't have to be afraid of the future. You can take risks because you walk by faith and not by sight.

You Can Miss God's Plan

But you can miss God's plan. You can miss God's plan through apathy: you just don't care or don't care enough. You have to be looking, and you have to be watching. God will show you, but He's not necessarily going to knock you over the head. Ideally you don't have to get knocked over the head. I pray this prayer all the time: "God, no need to put me in the hospital. No need to bring all this hardship into my life. I'm listening, I'm watching" You can have it the other way, but I'm going to try to pass on those things as much as is possible.

You can miss God's plan through ignorance: you aren't seeking it. You're not trying to learn and you're not trying to listen. And if you are not trying to learn and you're not trying to listen, it doesn't matter how much God communicates: you are not going to get it. You need to say, "I'm listening and I'm ready to learn. Teach me your ways, show me your plan."

There is another way you can miss God's plan—rebellion: you want to do what you want to do. You don't want to do what God wants you to do. There is a story in the Bible of a man named Jonah. He rebelled against God's plan for his life. It did not go well for him. He ended up inside a whale. You think it's scary to believe God for your comeback? Let me tell you what is really scary—running from God. You don't want to run from God. You want to run to God and allow him to work in your life. Your future is under God's control. And He is faithful to fulfill what He says He will do. What He starts, He finishes.

God is a finisher. He doesn't have a plan, starts it, and then moves on. He has a plan, He works the plan, and the plan gets done. God is with you each step of the way. You never go into the future alone. God's Spirit is right there with you, right alongside of you. The Greek word *paraclete* is the word in the Bible for the Holy Spirit; it means "the one who comes alongside of you". God is with you. You don't have to be fearful because God is with you.

Is it scary to think about making a comeback? Yes, it is. How will you ever come back from your setback? How will your future ever be better? But is the future something that needs to be feared? Not if you are a follower of Christ, not if you choose faith! You don't have to be afraid. You don't have to be fearful. With God in your life, you can confidently move into a future that though uncertain to you, is most certainly known by God. Choose faith, trust God's plan, and have your comeback.

REASONS FOR 2 A SETBACK

Life is full of setbacks. You cannot avoid them no matter what you do, no matter who you are; even Tiger Woods knows that. You can, however, avoid taking a step back when obstacles come. The challenge is knowing how to overcome your setback. How do you overcome a job loss? How do you overcome health issues? How do you overcome divorce? How do you overcome financial problems? How do you overcome the loss of a loved one? How do you take a setback and make a comeback?

In 2001, *Sports Illustrated* published an article entitled, "Bouncing Back Big Time" where they listed their Top Ten Comebacks of All Time. You would think the comebacks would all have been sports-related, but they were not. In fact, the article listed Elvis Presley when he had his television special in 1968 and how that was the beginning of his comeback in popularity. The article talked about how President Truman beat Thomas Dewey in the 1948 presidential election when Dewey was favored in all the polls. Some newspapers had already printed that Dewey was the new president, but Truman made a great comeback, winning the presidency. The article also mentioned Japan and Germany making great comebacks from their World War II defeats, reviving their economies and regaining their world-leader status. However, sports comebacks were included, of course, listing Michael Jordan returning to basketball after retirement and his baseball career to win more championships, and Muhammad Ali coming back after several years out of boxing to take back the heavyweight title.

The Greatest Comebacks of All Time

All of those comebacks were not their number-one comeback of all time, however. *Sports Illustrated* said that the top comeback of all time was Jesus Christ's resurrection from the dead. It was a great victory—the ultimate victory. From the ultimate setback of death, Jesus came back to life and proved his victory over death. If you doubt the veracity of Jesus' resurrection, consider some evidence. In ancient courts, a woman could not be a witness; only the testimony of a man was accepted. Yet the first witnesses of Jesus' resurrection were women. If it were just a fanciful story, why would the gospel writers have used women as witnesses?

The resurrection cannot be a myth because it does not fit the characteristics of a myth. Myths are developed over time, but the story of Jesus' resurrection was written within twenty years of its happening and was known orally many years before that. Also, Christians never venerated the site of Jesus' death. Rather, they focused on the tomb where he had arisen. In addition, there were approximately five hundred witnesses who saw Jesus after his resurrection. How could that many people all have the story wrong?

The reality is Jesus was raised from the dead, and because of Jesus' victory over death and sin, we can experience forgiveness and eternal life. We can overcome any setback through the strength God gives. You can make any comeback with the power that is available through Jesus Christ.

Though comebacks are absolutely possible, it is important to understand and identify the reasons for your setback. You must begin with the setback before you can get to the comeback. You have to understand and identify what caused your setback. There are numerous potential causes for setbacks, but I believe there are only a few main reasons for setbacks. It is absolutely essential for you to understand what those reasons are because, before you can launch a comeback, you need to understand why you had the setback in the first place.

We need a comeback as a country. The idea to write on comebacks first started percolating in my mind several years ago as I was thinking about how much America needs to come back from its financial collapse and all the problems it has created. I also thought about the challenges that exist in people's lives that point to the need for a comeback. If you don't need a comeback today, you will at some juncture. You can never get too far away from the setbacks of life.

We Experience Unexpected Circumstances

So what are these reasons for a setback? The first reason is this: we experience unexpected circumstances. We need look no further than the devastating earthquake that hit Haiti in 2010.

The people of Haiti have had all kinds of problems and challenges throughout the years, but one thing they have not had to deal with is earthquakes. They have dealt with hurricanes. They have dealt with enormous political issues and many other systemic issues in their culture and in their government. But it had been two hundred years since they had an earthquake that caused significant damage. Now this country had suffered a horrific earthquake in, of all places, the most populated area of the entire country—the capital city.

We in America also experienced an unexpected circumstance called the Great Recession. Who saw it coming? There are a lot of smart people who have graduate degrees in finance and whose life's work is to monitor the economy, yet they missed it. They didn't see it coming. How is it that we fell into such an unprecedented financial challenge? You may have lost your job and never saw it coming. If you thought there was going to be a problem, you never thought it would be as bad as it became.

Unexpected circumstances will come into your life. But although unexpected, it is still very important to not *dwell* on them but *acknowledge* them. Some of you may have trouble admitting, "Yeah, I've had a setback," or "I'm in the middle of a setback," but you don't have to take a step back because you've had a setback. You can take your setback and turn it into a comeback. However, it is important to acknowledge the setback and be honest with yourself about your situation.

When the NFL named Tom Brady as its Comeback Player of the Year, I was blown away. The guy who has had more success in professional football than anyone else over the last several years is now the Comeback Player of the Year. He had won three Super Bowl championships and had set the record for most touchdowns ever thrown in one season. How could Tom Brady be Comeback Player of the Year? How could someone that good *need* a comeback? Well, when someone lands on their knee in the wrong way and they miss an entire season because of injury, they need a comeback. Sometimes things happen that are unexpected.

I will never forget when one of the men in our church came to me a number of years ago and said, "Pastor Rick, I need to talk to you, and I need to talk to you right now."

"Okay," I said. "What's going on?"

"I came home from a business trip and my wife was gone."

"What do you mean 'gone'?"

"I mean her stuff is gone, and she's gone. I've called her and there is no answer."

I asked him if he had seen this coming, and he said he had not. They were newly married. He thought everything was fine, but apparently it was not.

Life has a way of throwing you curveballs. You go to the doctor. You think you just have a little something wrong. They do a few tests, and the result is totally unexpected. Now you find yourself in a completely different place in life. Unexpected circumstances happen.

Even if circumstances are beyond your control, you can still control your comeback. You can control how you will launch yourself out of the setback and into the comeback, and that is very important to understand at the setback stage. It is crucial to understand that you have to acknowledge the setback, but you don't have to accept it. Instead, you look forward to the comeback. We won't allow unexpected circumstances—things that are beyond our control—to dictate to us what our future is going to be. We decide what our life is going to be like, the happiness that we are going to have, and that a comeback will happen.

We Make Bad Decisions

There is another reason why we experience setbacks: we make bad decisions—sometimes ones we can't get around. Proverbs 14:8–12 says:

> Wise people have enough sense to find their way, but stupid fools get lost. Fools don't care if they are wrong, but God is pleased when people do right. No one can really know how sad or happy you are. The tent of a good person stands longer than the house of someone evil. You may think you are on the right road and still end up dead.

What Proverbs is saying is that we need wisdom to understand life's challenges, as wisdom is knowledge applied to life. "Fools don't care if they are wrong, but God is pleased when people do right." We can make decisions that end up being wrong, and we have to acknowledge that. We can't go around pretending our foolish decisions haven't caused a setback. It's disappointing and very humbling, but it shouldn't keep us from owning the reason for our setback.

Sometimes when you don't take care of yourself physically, you end up at the doctor. A logical progression of not taking care of the body God has given you is that you end up with a health setback. Health problems can be unexpected, but many are not because of circumstances beyond your control. You could have controlled them, but you decided not to.

I think a great way to learn control when it comes to diet is to fast. There are many good reasons for fasting. One reason is Jesus told us to fast. He did not say *if* you fast, He said *when* you fast (Matthew 6:16). A second reason for fasting is that you will have spiritual experiences like you won't have in any other way. And third, fasting will bring blessing and favor into your life in a special way.

It is also helpful to understand why God chose fasting. The desire for food is natural, normal, and powerful, so giving up food helps you to understand the influence that it has over your life. Seeing some of the choices you make with your diet and the way you use food for comfort is very illuminating.

The number-one reason why people file bankruptcy is because of medical bills. As the Bible says, "You may think you are on the right road and still end up dead." Unexpected circumstances can adversely affect your finances.

After medical bills, the reasons why people have filed bankruptcy and have financial problems are all lumped into the category of bad decisions. The economic downturn was unexpected, but some are suffering because of bad financial decisions they made. Some chose to buy a house that was beyond anything they needed and thus purchased a home that was too much house for too much money. Others made decisions to live beyond their means, used credit cards to purchase what they wanted, and then found themselves in way too much debt. Many used their home equity line as free spending, thinking the value of their home would always increase and cover the amount.

Other setbacks, such as divorce, can be the result of bad decision-making. Perhaps you did not go through premarital counseling, or you did not take enough time to get to know the person before you made what is supposed to be a lifelong commitment. Or you may have ignored the advice of your parents and friends.

You will never make a comeback until you first acknowledge the setback and then your responsibility in making the bad decision in the first place.

We Fail to Plan

There is another reason for a setback: we fail to plan. You know the motto, "When you fail to plan, you plan to fail." Look again at what the Bible says, "Wise people have enough sense to find their way, but stupid fools get lost." You may say, "I don't know if I like the Bible calling me stupid." Well, sometimes the truth hurts. People who are wise have a plan, have a path, have a direction! And when you don't, you can find yourself suffering a setback.

You have a setback because you didn't know where you were going, and then you wonder, "Why am I here?" You have got to face that your lack of planning has now created a setback in your life. Without a plan you are adrift, and then you open yourself up to continual setbacks in your life.

When Henry Ford built the first automobile, he forgot to include a reverse gear. It was an incredible invention that has changed our world forever, but you can't always drive forward. But Henry bounced back; he added a reverse gear, and then things went very well for him and his car company. Like Henry Ford, you too can bounce back from your lack of planning, but it is absolutely crucial to understand the importance of direction and planning. And that is what makes following Christ so valuable.

To have a comeback without God's help is much more difficult. If you follow Him, you have a built-in plan for your life, which makes life so much easier and simpler. You are then able to understand His purpose and plan for your life. As a matter of fact, following Jesus is a continuous unfolding of God's plan for your life.

God has a plan unique for you; it is not like anyone else's in the world. In order to discover it, you must follow Him. He will then take you places, both expected and unexpected—a marvelous ride that wards off setbacks. There are enough unexpected things that happen in life, so we don't need to make it any harder. We no longer need to cooperate with the challenges of life. If we plan and follow God's plan, we will find ourselves far ahead of the game.

We Ignore God's Instructions

Another reason for setbacks: we ignore God's instructions. What does the Bible say? "The tent of a good person stands longer than the house of someone evil." When you follow God's instructions, you will not do evil.

The Bible is our owner's manual for life. I recently had a problem with one of my cars. I looked up the section in the owner's manual that dealt with the problem and did what it said to do. Because I followed the instructions, I avoided a potentially costly repair. Some don't like to use the owner's manual, though, because they think they can figure things out for themselves.

This is how some of you have gotten into the setback you are currently in because you are not following the Manual, the Bible. Meanwhile, the people who are following the Bible's instructions are avoiding setbacks. They are reading the number-one bestseller of all time and taking advantage of the greatest wealth of wisdom available. But if you don't follow its instructions, you can end up in a setback position. Then you have to get real with yourself and acknowledge your responsibility. When you don't obey God, when you go against his teachings, you end up in a setback.

Neil White tells his story in the book, *In the Sanctuary of Outcasts*. His setback involved losing his business and ending up in prison for check fraud. But the Louisiana prison he went to was not an ordinary prison; it was the last home in the United States for people disfigured by leprosy. Yet even though he had gone bankrupt, left thirty of his employees without jobs, cost bankers a million dollars, and betrayed his wife and children, he still did not acknowledge his wrongdoing. Not until he was in a sanctuary for outcasts who could not hide their disfigurement could he see his own. His desire to be successful and admired had caused him to ignore the reality that he was a thief. Though his disfigurement was on the inside, he still needed to accept that his stealing caused his setback. He had ignored his own morals and religious teachings; only by seeing the truth, which he finally did, was he able to make a comeback.

If you are going to have a comeback, you must follow God's principles. If you want to avoid a setback, you must follow God's instructions, which is not advice that you can take or leave. God's principles are the way to live your life; following God's instructions is the way your life will turn out for the best, and God's plan for you will be fulfilled. This is how you can have happiness and peace.

It is not enough to know the principles; you must do something more—you must put them into practice. And when you do, you will avoid setbacks.

You Can Avoid Setbacks

You can avoid setbacks in life—not all, but many. You can recognize and understand the reasons why you have setbacks. The Bible says, "Fools don't care if they are wrong!" If you don't care, get used to a life of setbacks and disappointment. But I don't think you want that or you would not be reading this book.

Sometimes we have setbacks—and when we do, we need to identify the reason why, which is the beginning of a marvelous comeback in our lives. The setback doesn't mean we have to take a step back, nor does it mean we have to stay in the setback position.

You are now in position to have a marvelous comeback.

LESSONS 3 FROM A SETBACK

There is a man from Richmond, Virginia, named John Kuester, a high school basketball star who received a scholarship to the University of North Carolina. After his basketball-playing days were over, he entered into the field of coaching. By the age of twenty-seven, he had his first head coaching job at Boston University, where he coached for a couple of years before going on to George Washington University and coaching for another five years. But when he was thirty-five, he had a losing season and got fired. For the first time in his life, John was without a job. In an interview with John O'Conner in the *Richmond Times-Dispatch*, he says this about it, "I was unemployed and wondering what I should do. I had two avenues to go. One was to look to do something different for an occupation. The other was to get better at my craft of being a coach."

John got hired by the Boston Celtics, but not as a coach. After a number of years, he eventually became a key assistant coach. In 2009, at the age of fifty-four, John got another opportunity to be a head coach, this time with the Detroit Pistons. Here is what he says about his experience, "You are going to have setbacks. But how are you going to handle those things and learn from them? You need to learn from those kinds of situations and that is what I did."

John had a setback, turned it around, had a comeback, and landed a prestigious job. How did that happen? He learned the lessons from his setback.

Before the comeback, you have to look closely at the setback. A setback should be dissected, not discarded. Yet many want to discard the setback. They want to pretend it never happened and move on. No one wants to relive the disappointment, the failure, and the shortcoming of a setback.

Look for the Lesson

In order to have a comeback, you must look for the lesson. Many try to push the setback behind them as quickly as possible, which is precisely why so many go from setback to setback to setback. I believe God's desire is for everyone to have a comeback. But in order to do so, there are certain things you must do. And if you are unwilling to look for the lessons in the setback, you will never enjoy a comeback.

Some want to point their finger at God and say, "You've done me wrong. You never bless me; I never end up on the right side of things." The reality is before you turn away from or blame God for the setback, you need to ask yourself if God is trying to tell you something. Ecclesiastes 10:8–10 says:

> If you dig a pit, you might fall in. If you break down a wall, a snake might bite you. You could even get hurt by chiseling a stone or chopping a log. If you don't sharpen your ax, it will be harder to use. If you are smart, you will know what to do.

If you are smart, you will ask yourself, "Is there a lesson here?" Maybe there is, or maybe God is trying to show you something. Before you run away from or try to bury it, before you try to stop thinking about it, remember that God may have gotten your attention for a reason. The setback is so that you might sharpen your ax and be smarter the next time.

There are stupid people, and there are smart people. What's the difference? It is not IQ. Actually the Bible's definition isn't about innate intelligence. When the Bible talks about smart or stupid, it is referring to wisdom, which is the application of knowledge.

All of us can receive knowledge that we can either apply or not. The Bible says if you are smart, you will know what to do. You will know that you need to be careful when you are chiseling a stone or when you are chopping down a tree. You need to be wise about the things you do. And if you hurt yourself the first time, you will make sure to learn the lesson for the next time. But you need to look for the lesson. Whatever has happened, whatever your setback may be, you need to look for the lesson. If you think there is no lesson, you need to look harder and peer deeper.

A couple will come to me and say, "We want to get married. We have both been divorced and have fallen in love, so we want to get remarried." I have a premarital process I use with couples to properly prepare them for a lifelong commitment, but the reality is that sixty percent of second marriages end in divorce. What is going on?

People are not looking for the lesson. They are not looking for what they can learn from their first failed marriage that will keep them from experiencing the same setback again. If you failed the first time, you want to make sure it does not happen a second time.

You can blame other people. You can think it is just bad luck. You can try to not think about it at all. Or you can look for the lesson. A good approach would be to ask, "Is there anything I can take away from this setback?"

You lost your job. Is it downsizing or the economy? It could be when it came time to downsize; there was a process and a choice to be made. Maybe you didn't keep up your skills the way you should have. Possibly you were hard to work with, or you did not work hard enough. This is hard stuff to look at, but you need to look for the lesson.

There was a man named Wallace Johnson, who you probably never heard of. Sixty years ago when he was forty years old, he got fired from his job. When he told his wife, she said, "What are we going to do now?" He said, "I want to take a mortgage out on our home. I want to get money together and start my own construction company." Within five years he was making a lot of money. He says this: "At the time it happened, I didn't understand why I was fired. Later, I saw that it was God's wondrous plan for me. It was God's plan for me to get me onto a different path and a different way."

You may not know who Wallace Johnson is, but you may have heard of the company he founded—Holiday Inn. By the time he passed away, he was a multimillionaire.

There Are Many Different Lessons

God can do amazing things and bring about marvelous comebacks, but first you must uncover the lesson from the setback. You thought you had arrived, and possibly that is what happened to you. You got to a place of success where you didn't care how you treated other people, or you didn't care about certain decisions you made because you had "arrived." There is the lesson of the whale: "Just when you get to the top and you start to blow, you can get harpooned."

Maybe you are a fearful person. You got afraid and anxious and didn't want to take the necessary risks. Maybe the lesson for you is to stop letting fear dictate your life and future. Stop making fear-based decisions and start making faith-based decisions.

Or your setback may be that you quit. You decided that you could not keep going, that things were too difficult, so you simply gave up. The lesson for you is to persevere through the difficulties. Keep at it, because eventually you will succeed. For everyone who has a setback, there are lessons to be learned.

I read on *msnbc.com* about a woman named Lucia Del Barto from Arizona, who shared what happened to her in the Great Recession. She said, "If it weren't for the economy going so bad, I'd still be blowing money left and right and not even trying to better myself with an education. I'm grateful because of the recession. The recession gave me a new opportunity, hope, and purpose."

Not many people are thanking God for the Recession. Yet here is a woman who saw the Recession as a wakeup call to look for the lesson. And for her the lesson was to stop blowing money and to get an education, thus providing a more solid and secure foundation for her future.

Learn from the Lesson

God can use the tough, difficult, and challenging experiences of life for your good if you are willing to look for the lesson. But many people want to throw the lessons aside or brush them off rather than face them head-on and ask the hard questions. "Is there a lesson here for me in this setback? What is it I can learn from this?" You should be looking for the lesson in your setback, and you need to learn that lesson. It is one thing to look for the lesson, but it is another thing to actually learn from it. Despite setbacks, you can learn from them. And in learning from them, you can fashion a marvelous comeback.

I love Walt Disney. I have read a number of biographies about him. He fascinates me for his creative energy and marvelous visionary leadership. What you might not know is that he experienced seven very disappointing setbacks in his life. But Walt Disney always looked for the lesson and learned from the lesson. Therefore, he didn't repeat his mistakes. When you think of him, you think of the movies and the theme parks. His name is on a television and a radio network. The Disney name is the gold standard for creativity.

The lesson means nothing if we don't learn it and make the appropriate change. You don't need to wonder why so many people never have a comeback: it is because they are unwilling to learn the lesson.

Warren Buffett, one of the richest people in the world, often talks about one of his early setbacks when he was not accepted into Harvard. He says, "Setbacks teach lessons that carry you along. You learn that a temporary defeat is not a permanent one. In the end, it can be an opportunity." Buffett used what he learned from his setback early in life to become an incredible financial success.

Learn from the Great Recession

Since the Great Recession caused so much financial challenge, it might be worthwhile to look at the possible lessons to be learned.

What can we learn from the experience that we have been through? I think the first thing we can learn is to live within our means. If you live within your means, you don't get into debt. And if you don't get into debt, you won't find yourself so negatively impacted by the loss of a job or a decrease in your income.

For a number of years, some folks were buying homes that were beyond what they even needed—for example, a four thousand-square-foot home with five bedrooms for a family of four. A good way to know you are buying a house that is too big for you is when you can't even furnish it. If they had purchased the three thousand-square-foot, four-bedroom house, it could have cost $150,000 less. And it is that extra money each month for the mortgage that is causing financial hardship. Live within your means; that is a good lesson to learn.

Debt can be very destructive. Having an extra payment or payments every month limits you financially. Instead of investing or saving money, you have to pay your debts, and the amount of interest you pay can be more than your original debt. The pressure and stress that debt places on you is simply not worth it. Getting out and staying out of debt frees you up financially, so a financial setback will not destroy you.

Here is another lesson: know your financial basics. Too many people do not know basic financial principles necessary to succeed. These basics include having a budget, debt reduction, investing, real estate, insurance, and giving. Having basic knowledge on home mortgages (interest rates, closing costs, fixed versus adjustable rates, etc.) could have spared thousands from unwise home purchases that have created a huge financial setback for so many. Knowing your financial basics can help you navigate through challenging times and avoid a painful setback.

What other lessons can we learn? That nothing lasts forever. Prices for real estate can go up and up, but eventually they come down. The stock market can rocket to record levels, but a correction will eventually lower it. Growth is great, but nothing grows forever. McDonalds had twenty-five years where they increased their profits each year, one hundred successive quarters of increasing profits, but eventually even that ended.

It is foolish to think we can experience only good financial times and never have setbacks. Good times never last forever, and neither do the bad. Learn the lessons.

Don't Make the Same Mistakes Again

Learn the lesson so you don't repeat the same mistake. You may not want to revisit your setback. Everything in you may never want to think about it again, but you need to look for the lesson or lessons. You need to learn. You don't want to go through the same pain again, and you don't have to. You don't need to repeat the same mistakes again. You can learn so you can go from the setback to the comeback. Put into practice the wisdom that you have learned through defeat and failure. Use the knowledge and the feedback to forge a better way to go, a better route to take, a better path to your future.

Suppose you make a big mistake on your job. How do you regain credibility from your setback? You own up to your mistake. If you are at fault, don't make excuses or take a defensive stance. Go to your boss and share the lessons you have learned from the experience. If you can make amends or correct the mistake, do it. If you cannot do anything to change the situation, take responsibility for putting a process into place to undo the damage if possible and keep the mistake from happening again.

Rod Blagojevich, the former governor of Illinois, experienced quite a setback. In 2011 he was convicted of seventeen counts in a corruption case involving his role in filling the open Senate seat of Barack Obama. Blagojevich has gone from being governor to a convicted felon. He had these poignant words to say after his conviction, "Among the many lessons that I've learned from this whole experience is to try to speak a little bit less."

Psalm 34:17 says, "When his people pray for help, he listens and rescues them from their troubles. The Lord is there to rescue all who are discouraged and have given up hope. The Lord's people may suffer a lot, but he will always bring them safely through." Here is the good news: God will help you. He will bring you from a setback to a comeback. "The Lord's people may suffer a lot, but he will always bring them safely through." After you have looked for the lesson and learned from it, after you have done your part, here is what God says to you: "I will help you. I will rescue you. I will bring you from a setback to a comeback."

That is God's message to you. That is the God we serve. If you don't have a relationship with God, this is one of the reasons why you want to have one with him through Jesus Christ. If you have a relationship with God, you can

stand on the promise that God takes you from setl
comebacks.

God wants us to pause long enough to look for the
lesson in the setback. He wants us to take enough time to
learn the lessons we need to learn so we don't experience
yet another setback. Then we can move in God's direction
for our lives—a positive, growing, uplifting direction God
wants for each of us.

READY FOR A COMEBACK

Clyde the cat lived with his family in Hobart, Tasmania, an island off the coast of Australia, and went missing when he was about one year old. Three years later, a veterinarian in Cloncurry a city in the Australian Outback contacted the family, informing them that he had found Clyde. From Tasmania to Cloncurry is about twenty-four hundred miles, one hundred eighty-five of which is over the Bass Strait. The Outback is then one thousand plus miles into the middle of Australia.

Clyde had an implanted microchip, which is how the vet knew to contact the family. A nurse had found Clyde hanging around her hospital and had taken him in as her pet. When she had to go on a trip, she left Clyde with her vet, which is when the vet found the microchip.

Through that microchip, they were able to discover the cat belonged to the Sullivan family. So Clyde the cat had a twenty-four-hundred-mile comeback to be reunited with his family. The little girl who owned him said, "It's pretty special to have him back. He seems as if he was never gone. He doesn't seem to be surprised by what has happened."

How does a cat end up twenty-four hundred miles away from home, including traveling over one hundred eighty-five miles of sea, and then become reunited with his family? I don't know that we will ever get the answer to that question, but I will tell you this much: if a cat can have a comeback, I am sure you can have one, too.

Change Is Required

Are you ready for a comeback? Are you ready to move out of the setback and into a comeback? The comeback hinges on one word: *change.*

If you keep doing what you have always done, you will keep getting what you've always gotten. If you want a comeback, you are going to have to change something. A setback says to you, "Change what you are doing." If you have had a setback in your marriage, your finances, or your health, you have got to change what you are doing. Otherwise, things are going to remain the same; there will be no comeback.

When President Obama gave the State of the Union address, he said, "We've had some setbacks as a country." He then said, "I've had some setbacks." That is an acknowledgment of reality that is true for all of us in some way. Now the question is, "How are we going to have a comeback?"

The comeback will happen because of change. Things have to be different. If you want to have a comeback, you have to be willing to change. You have to be willing to do things differently from what you've done up to this point. Being ready for a comeback means you are ready to change.

There is a fascinating comeback story in the Bible, but it is a somewhat unknown comeback story because you have to dig to find it. The story is about a man named Mark, recorded in Mark 14:50–52: "All of Jesus' disciples ran off and left him. One of them was a young man who was wearing only a linen cloth. And when the men grabbed him, he left the cloth behind and ran away naked." The next part of the story is found in the book of Acts 13:13: "Paul and the others left Paphos and sailed to Perga, which is in Pamphylia. But John left them and went back to Jerusalem." The final part of the story is found in 2 Timothy 4:11: "Only Luke has stayed with me. Mark can be very helpful to me, so please find him and bring him with you."

Mark also went by his first name, John. Acts 12:12 says "When this dawned on him, he went to the house of Mary, the mother of John, also called Mark." Some people go by their middle name, not their first name, and John Mark did this. We discovered my eldest son did this as well. He is named Matthew Graham, and we have always called him Matt. When he went away to college at West Point, there were so many Matts that he decided to be called by Graham. When we went to one of his first football games, people were talking to us about "Graham," and my wife and I were looking at each other, wondering whom they were talking about. After the game, we asked our son and he told us that at West Point he is called Graham.

So John Mark wrote the gospel of Mark, which tells us something that the gospels of Matthew, Luke, and John don't. Only in Mark are we told that there was a young man who ran away naked when Jesus was arrested. Since Mark included that information in his gospel without naming himself, we can deduce that the naked guy who fled was Mark.

Useless to Useful

We are introduced to Mark initially in the book of Acts as a coward. When things get tough, he runs. He is such a coward that even when people grab him and his clothes, he runs away, leaving his clothes behind. Years later, we are reintroduced to this guy again in Acts 13:5, "When they arrived at Salamis, they proclaimed the word of God in the Jewish synagogues. John was with them as their helper." Now he is called John. Sometimes he is called Mark, sometimes he is called John, but it is the same guy—John Mark.

The story here is that two men named Paul and Barnabas are going on a missionary journey. By the way, Barnabas and (John) Mark are cousins. They are going into dangerous territories, and if you were to read the rest of chapter 13, you would see the kind of danger they encountered. Paul and Barnabas leave, and Mark comes along as their helper, their assistant. Just a few verses later, in Acts 13:13, we read, "John Mark left them and went back to Jerusalem." So fifteen years earlier Mark was a coward who fled, leaving Jesus behind. Now, in a new endeavor with his cousin Barnabas and Paul, he quits again when things get tough. He was a coward before, and now he is also a quitter. These are setbacks, major setbacks in this young man's life.

We read in 1 Peter 5:13, "So does my son Mark." Ten years later, the apostle Peter considers Mark to be like a son to him. So something has happened. The coward and the quitter had quite a comeback. He is now seen by one of the great leaders of the early church as someone so valuable that he is like a son to him. In fact, the gospel of Mark, although written by Mark, is actually Peter's eyewitness account of the life of Jesus. Peter spent three years with Jesus and then shared all his knowledge with Mark, who wrote it as one of the gospels.

Then in Colossians 4:10, the same Paul who Mark quit on before lists several people as fellow workers with him, "And Mark, one of my fellow workers." The guy who was a coward and a quitter is now considered to be a fellow worker with the apostle Paul. Then 2 Timothy 4:11 says, "Only Lucas stayed with me. Mark can be very helpful to me, so please bring him with you." This man who was a coward and had a setback, was a quitter and had another setback, has now had such a comeback that the apostle Paul believes Mark could be very helpful and wants him brought to Paul.

What happened to this young man? How did he go from terrible setbacks to this marvelous comeback? There is no information in the Bible about how this happened, but here is what I deduce from this story: something changed in Mark so dramatically that he overcame these terrible setbacks. What could have destroyed a person—"I'm a coward. I walked out on Jesus. I'm such a quitter. I quit on Paul and Barnabas. I have failed, and I have fallen short in so many ways"—did not destroy Mark. He made an incredible comeback. Peter and Paul, the two great leaders of the early church, both believed he was a valuable person.

Change Your Mind

An incredible, marvelous change took place in Mark's life. If you are going to go from setback to comeback, there must be a change in your life. And the change must be a change of mind.

A change of mind happens when you receive new information and gain new knowledge. Part of that new knowledge is gained through the setback. We have covered the information in learning the lessons in the previous chapter.

With any new knowledge, there is resistance to changing your mind. I'm in the business of helping people become who God wants them to be, and I've seen this resistance firsthand. The resistance is mostly fear of the unknown. The way you overcome fear is with belief. You believe that the change can happen, that it can be done. You trust that you can be different and that you can be better. You can do it this time because you know more, you are wiser, and you have opened yourself up to the principles that will lead to a comeback.

A few years ago, members of a tribe in South America kept dying prematurely, so some scientists were brought in to find out why. They discovered that the people were getting a specific disease from insects that lived inside the clay adobe walls of their huts. It was great to have this new information, but the question for the tribe was what to do.

One possible solution was they could move to another place where those insects did not live. Thus they would no longer get the disease and no longer die prematurely.

Another possibility was to tear down the existing huts and rebuild them, using an insecticide in the clay that would repel the insects so they would not get into the homes. Thus the huts would no longer make the people sick, and they wouldn't die of the disease.

A third option was to remain the same and continue dying prematurely.

Now, of those three options, which one would you opt for? You may not know which of the first two options to choose, but anyone would know the third option is not really an option. To do nothing would mean continued early death, so action needed to be taken. But the South American tribe chose to do nothing. They decided to stay where they were and live in the same huts they lived in.

We can look at those people and think, *Why would they not change?* But before we judge the poor, uneducated tribesmen in another land, we might want to ask ourselves, "What is it *we* are refusing to change?"

How many setbacks do you have to have before you are ready for a comeback? A comeback means change, and the first thing that must change is your mind.

Change Your Heart

After a change of mind, there must be a change of heart. A change of heart is the result of a new attitude, when you decide that your way or mode of thinking (which is the definition of an *attitude*) is going to change. You determine that you are going to see things from a different perspective. When you see things from a different perspective and you think differently about yourself, others, and God, you then have a change of heart.

It is amazing how you can move from a setback to a comeback when you change your attitude. Some people have never had the comeback they should have had, and the reason is because they refused to change their attitude. A negative attitude will never lead to a comeback. Never.

You may know the name Lee Child. He has written twenty-one books, including the incredible best-selling *Jack Reacher* series. In fact, two of his books have now been made into successful movies starring Tom Cruise. He initially got into the motion picture business and spent the early part of his career doing television and making movies and was very happy.

For fifteen years, Lee worked in a family-owned company where everyone was actually treated like family. But then the company was purchased by a larger company, which happens all the time in business. One of the first things the new owner did was get rid of the original owners and then the employees, which included Lee. He says, "I was thirty-nine years old and soon to be forty. Not a great age to be unemployed. If there was ever a time to make a change, this was it."

Lee looked at his big setback and decided what he really wanted to do: write novels. So he had to figure out a way to support himself and his family while he wrote. In order to do this, his wife had to go back into the workplace and his teenage daughter had to waitress to help the family get by. In a *Parade* article, he goes on to say this, "The point is this: if you're fired at forty, it's not about the hurt, it's not about the betrayal, it's not about the fear—it's about the opportunity." That kind of attitude led to his career comeback.

Many people lost their jobs in the Great Recession, but their attitude about it was not one of opportunity. Rather, it was one of never getting as good a job again or making as much money. The setback does involve hurt, anger, and betrayal. However, if you're going to get out of the setback and into the comeback, it's going to be about your attitude. You need to begin thinking differently. You must open yourself up to new possibilities, new opportunities, and new experiences. But if your attitude doesn't change and you don't have a change of heart, it won't happen.

Mitch Albom tells the story of a man named Tom Smallwood who got laid off from General Motors two days before Christmas in 2008. He applied for other jobs but received no response. He was married, had a one-year-old daughter, and was out of job options. So Tom decided to make a significant change: he would pursue his boyhood dream of becoming a professional bowler.

Tom started going to the bowling alley every day, and in May he entered the Pro Bowlers Association Tour Trials. He bowled nine games a day for five days, and when it was all over, he had qualified for a tour exemption, which meant a guaranteed spot and a minimum paycheck at each PBA event for a year. He says, "It was like someone said, 'Congratulations, you got a new job.'" Tom saw losing his job as an opportunity to pursue a dream, one he never would have considered had he not lost his job.

But Tom's story does not end there; it gets better. One year after he lost his job with General Motors, he was competing in the PBA World Championship in Wichita, Kansas. He made it all the way to the final, and his opponent was the reigning PBA Player of the Year, Wes "Big Nasty" Malott. The match came down to the final frame, and Tom threw a strike to win—and he did. He won $50,000—more money than he ever made in one year at his old job.

Tom says about the whole experience, "Getting laid off was one of the worst things that ever happened to me. But it led to the best result." Tom's fantastic comeback was the result of his willingness to change, to think differently, and to explore new opportunities.

Change Your Future

There is another change that must happen: you must change your future. But just how do you change your future?

You change your future through commitment. You change your mind through knowledge, you change your heart through attitude, and you change your future through commitment. You choose to be committed to your comeback. Everybody wants a comeback, but the difference between people who have setbacks and then comebacks and people who have setbacks and no comebacks is commitment.

You are ready for a comeback when you commit to change. Not when you *want* to change, not when you think you *should* change, and not when you *talk about* changing, but when you *commit* to change. There is a phrase I quote often, "Successful people are simply ordinary people who make commitments others are unwilling to make." I believe that because I have witnessed it over and over again in my life and leadership. When you make commitments, your future changes for the better.

To have a comeback, you simply must be committed to your comeback. You must believe you will have a comeback and stay committed to the process however long it may take. You can change your future, and that change will always involve at its most basic level a willingness to commit. When you commit to do what has to be done to make the changes that need to be made in your life, you are ready for a comeback.

Of all the changes a person could make, one is preeminent and will lead you to a comeback in your life. The change is so significant that it is called being born again (John 3:3). Every person is born physically, and every person needs to be born spiritually, which is what it means to be born again. There has to be a point you come to where you say, "I know I am far from perfect, and a perfect God can't accept an imperfect person like me." You must have enough change of heart to say, "I need God's help in order to become the person I should be. In order to have the comeback I need to have, I must have God's help." And then you must make a commitment, where you say, "God, I commit to following you. I receive your forgiveness through Jesus Christ's death on the cross for my sins. I commit my life to you and to a relationship with you, and I will live my life following your teachings and principles."

The Greatest Change of All

This fundamental change is necessary for every person because the Bible says, "All have sinned" (Romans 3:23). No one is perfect; everyone has sinned and fallen short of God's standard. So we all find ourselves in the same human condition. We must come to a place of change, and that foundational change will then guide all our other changes.

Have you ever made that commitment to God? Have you ever had that change experience in your life? If you haven't, here is how it can happen: you pray and tell God your desire for change. Prayer is our way of communicating with God. Pray, "I recognize that I am not perfect, and I know that I need to change. I ask you, Jesus, to come into my life and forgive me of all my past mistakes, failures, and sins. I commit myself to following you as you guide and direct my life. I ask this in your name, Jesus. Amen."

Now you are ready for your comeback.

COMPONENTS OF A COMEBACK

God specializes in do-overs. God specializes in start-overs. God specializes in new beginnings. God specializes in comebacks. If you have had a setback and want a comeback, God is your answer. Zephaniah 3:17 says:

The Lord your God wins victory after victory and is always with you. He celebrates and sings because of you. And he will refresh your life with his love.

God is always there to bring you to victory. He celebrates because of you. He will refresh you. He will restore you. Whatever has taken place, whatever the setback in your life, whether financial, the loss of a loved one, a health issue, or a job loss, God wants to bring you to a comeback.

I read in the newspaper about a guy who got shot. When the paramedics brought him into the emergency room, he was still awake and became really scared because the expressions on the faces of the nurses and the doctor told him that he was not going to make it. They asked him, "Are you allergic to anything?" He purposely paused to make sure they were all listening. Then he said, "Bullets. Now operate on me like I'm going to live!" And he did live. This man believed his comeback was possible, and he wanted the people attending to him to believe it, too.

Your comeback is possible, but certain key components must exist in your life. When they do, God will do his part.

Restore Your Confidence

Will you do your part? Will you do what you can do? If so, the first thing you can do is restore your confidence. You can choose to be confident.

Your confidence always takes a big hit when you have a setback. When you lose your job, it shakes you. When your spouse walks out the door, it rocks you. Setbacks have a way of affecting your confidence like nothing else, and confidence is crucial to a comeback. Confidence is the expectation that you will succeed and is the power that propels you to a comeback. You have to restore your confidence, your courage, and your edge. People who make comebacks are people who have restored their confidence.

Having confidence should come easier when you know the Bible is telling you that your God is going to win victory after victory and is always with you. You can base your confidence on the reality of who God is.

Confidence helps you to take advantage of new opportunities. Comebacks always come with new opportunities. People who stay in the setback, who allow the setback to become a step back, are people who watch opportunities go by without seizing them. They do not take advantage of these opportunities because they lack confidence. A lack of confidence keeps you from making the decisions you need to make.

Your comeback will be in part about opportunities and the decisions you make about those opportunities. Some people are so negatively impacted by their setbacks that they are paralyzed and cannot make new, better decisions.

David Duval was once the number-one ranked golfer in the world. He had plunged all the way to number 882 and needed to qualify just to play in the 2009 US Open at Bethpage Black. He was tied for the lead on the seventieth hole when his five-foot par putt caught the back of the lip and spun 180 degrees out the other side. He ended up finishing tied for second, his best finish on the PGA tour in eight years. Duval has experienced several setbacks, and I was impressed with his playing so well on such a difficult course in a major championship. But what amazed me most were his comments after the tournament. "I stand before you certainly happy with how I played but extremely disappointed in the outcome. I had no question in my mind I was going to win this golf tournament today." Duval definitely restored his confidence, opening the door to a comeback.

Everybody has setbacks; no one is immune. You cannot allow the setback to define you or rob you of your confidence to step into new beginnings and new opportunities. There is a do-over and a start-over for everyone!

God will be with you, but you have to take advantage of those opportunities and act on them. Action comes from confidence, from believing that you can have a comeback. And you absolutely, positively can.

Lose the Regret

Another key component is you must lose the regret. You cannot stay chained to the past. You must refuse to allow the past to determine your ability to have a comeback.

Do not permit guilt and condemnation to ruin your comeback. Don't say, "If only I had done this. If only I hadn't done that. If only I could go back." The past cannot be changed, but your future certainly can be. God's message is restoration, that comebacks are possible with

His help. It is the enemy of your soul who wants you to be filled with regret, focused on your past mistakes and failures. Romans 8:1 says, "There is therefore now no condemnation for those who are in Christ Jesus." If you have received God's forgiveness, there is no guilt. If you haven't, you need to receive that forgiveness.

You cannot change the past, but you can change the negative results of your past actions. You can decide that you will no longer have the same setbacks. Acting with wisdom gained from your setback can eliminate negative results. In the chapter, "Lessons from a Setback," I explained that there are lessons to be learned from a setback. But here is what is important to understand: you need to learn the lesson and then bury the experience. After you have extracted the lesson from the setback, stop replaying the experience.

I was talking with someone recently about one of my own setbacks. I have learned the lessons, but I have no desire to rehash the experience. Bury the experience. Refuse to allow the hurt, guilt, pain, and disappointment back into your life. Learn the lesson, move on, and lose the regret. Lose the kind of thinking that keeps you stuck in the setback because you can't let go of the past.

You can't make a comeback while dragging around the past. Unfortunately for many of us, there are people who will not let us forget. It isn't great to have those folks in your life. What I have learned is either they change or you have to get rid of them. This is not an easy thing to do, but if people keep talking about your past mistakes, they will hinder your comeback.

Refuse to dwell on the past. Lose the self-pity. Lose the regret. You are on your way to a comeback.

Have Forward Focus

A third component of a comeback is having a forward focus. You need to have a laserlike focus, and it must be in a forward direction.

If you focus on your setbacks, you have more setbacks. This is not what God wants for you. It is not God's plan for your life. You can get past the health challenge, you will get past this crushing loss, you will move past the relationship that broke apart. And you will do so by proceeding with new goals, new vision for a new future. Your forward focus will not allow you to stay in the setback position any longer.

God creates marvelous comebacks. He does them all the time. Here is a unique comeback story.

There was a young couple who wanted to be missionaries to Africa, a very noble desire. As they went through the qualifying process, the wife discovered that she had some medical issues that disqualified her from living in that kind of climate. The couple was devastated. Their dream had died. They longed to serve and help people, but now because of a health issue, they were stopped in their tracks and didn't know what to do.

The young man took over his father's side business in which he made grape juice for communion in church services. He built the business into the huge company that makes Welch's Grape Juice, Welch's Grape Jelly, and many other products, making a lot of money through which he financially supported African missions. This couple never was able to go to Africa, but what a difference they made through their giving. God turned their physical setback into a financial comeback.

You cannot have any more excuses or spend any more time placing blame. Your focus can only be forward. Don't look back. Jesus said, "No one who puts his hand to the plow and looks back is fit for the kingdom of God" (Luke 9:62). The kingdom of God is about focusing on the motion that takes you forward. Try balancing a bike just by sitting on it; you can't do it. But if you start moving, you can balance it perfectly. Forward movement—that is the kind of focus that leads to comebacks.

You miss one hundred percent of the shots you never take. You will never see results unless you make an attempt. Do you realize the best shooter makes fifty percent of his shots? If you could shoot fifty percent, you could have a long career playing basketball. That means half the time you make it, half the time you miss. In baseball, it is even better. If you are a .300 hitter, you can have a long and successful baseball career. A batting average of .300 means that out of ten at bats, you have three hits. It may not seem very impressive to those not familiar with baseball, but it is the standard for a good hitter. If you were to hit .400, you would be in very rare company in the history of baseball.

You must have focus and move forward in the direction of your comeback. If you do not, you will stay in the setback. No one wants to stay in the setback, yet so many people do. Too many people allow their setback to be a *step* back. Take one step forward and then another and another by having a laserlike focus on the future that God has planned for you.

Regain Your Momentum

There is another key component to a comeback: you must regain your momentum. Momentum is one of the best friends you could ever have. A well-known leader once told me, "Rick, momentum is your best friend because momentum will make you better than you could ever be."

Without momentum you will look worse than you really are, which is why setbacks are always about the loss of momentum. When you lose momentum, it is amazing how things can go in the wrong direction. Momentum is so powerful that when you shift from setback to comeback, you can shift the momentum in your life. It is just as the Bible says—you go from "victory after victory."

Momentum is emerging energy and limitless passion that positively fuels a comeback. What you need is to regain the momentum you once had, and that begins with concrete change and builds through positive experiences. That is how momentum works. You have a positive experience. Then you have another positive experience, which gives you a little more momentum that continues with clear direction, moving you down the path to your comeback. That leads you to a new start, a new beginning, a new goal, a new opportunity, and eventually a new future.

Momentum is mysterious, but I've tried to show how **concrete change** + **positive experiences** + **clear direction** = **momentum**. Momentum is your best friend when you are making a comeback. Nobody has ever had a comeback without it.

Once you get some momentum in your business, job, marriage, family, or health, it is amazing how it will fuel you right into a comeback. It is almost magical how it empowers you. Before you know it, you feel like you are gliding, and things are not so hard. Pieces start falling into place. It is easier to eat better and exercise. It is easier to be married to your spouse, and you start getting along better. You do the things you are supposed to do, and it gets easier. Momentum will fuel you right into a marvelous, powerful comeback.

My youngest son's football team was undefeated in the regular season of his junior year in high school and won the district championship. It was a dream season for a school in only its fourth season of varsity football. They won against teams they had never defeated before in thrilling fashion. My son ran for over eighteen hundred yards and scored twenty-one touchdowns.

They continued to win and went on to play for the regional championship on a bitterly cold night for Virginia, especially in November. They were playing another undefeated team, which was a very formidable opponent.

The game started off great with my son Wes having a long run, scoring a quick touchdown. But from that point on, everything went terribly wrong. They had turnovers, played poorly, and were behind 28–7 at halftime. We held out hope that they could turn it around after halftime, but the other team scored another touchdown, and they were now down 35–7. At that point, the game seemed lost for certain, and their dream season looked to be over.

Then my son's team scored a touchdown. The other team got possession and fumbled the ball. My son's team scored another touchdown, and the other team turned the ball over again. Momentum started kicking in; before we knew it, my son's team had scored four straight touchdowns, and the score was tied.

Each team then kicked a field goal, and the game went into overtime. In high school football, each team has an opportunity to score in overtime. The other team missed a very short field goal, and my son's team made theirs. They had come all the way back from a twenty-eight-point deficit and won the championship, the greatest comeback in Virginia high school football playoff history. The momentum they had in the second half simply propelled them to victory.

You know exactly the comeback you need, that you desire so much. God will be with every person who desires to come out of a setback and into a comeback. If you lose the regret, restore your confidence, and focus on your future, God will propel you into victory after victory. You can ride momentum straight into a comeback.

STEPS TO A COMEBACK

Setbacks don't define you. Everybody has setbacks. You're not a failure because you have setbacks; you are only a failure if you stop trying. I like the words to the song that says, "Impossible is not a word, it's just a reason not to try." The Bible says what is impossible with man is possible with God (Matthew 19:26). When people say it can't be done, it's an excuse for not trying. I remember these words from Hudson Taylor, a very famous missionary, "First, it's impossible. Then, it's difficult. Then, it's done."

When my older son, Matt, was a senior in high school, he wasn't getting the offers he wanted to play college football. I had taken him to a motivational seminar when he was twelve years old where he wrote, "My goal: to play college football and get a Division I scholarship." But it looked like it wasn't going to happen. I was very frustrated, and Matt was very unhappy; we thought his dream was done.

Then God gave me an idea: send the young man to prep school in my home state of Connecticut to get more exposure on a better team. His first game was a fantastic game, and I thought maybe he was going to have a comeback.

I couldn't go to all his games since I was in Virginia, but a few games after his first one, I went to see him play again. My dad and I were sitting with some of the parents, including one whose son had just signed with Notre Dame. Everyone was excited, and there was another father like me whose son was hoping to get a scholarship. In a period of just three plays, I saw my son run for an eighty-five-yard touchdown, get the ball again, score another touchdown, and then score again on a two-point conversion. The other dad turned to me and said, "I think if you take that film, your son will get a scholarship." Sure enough, that film was exactly what fulfilled my son's dream, and he went on to West Point to play football for Army.

God has such marvelous plans for you. God has a great comeback for your life. God does things even when the situation looks grim. God has a way of launching us from setbacks into comebacks. I know so many people who have come back from the premature birth of a baby, from financial problems, or from divorce. Comebacks are real and can happen in your life. I trust that hope has begun to be birthed in you.

Two Reflections on Setbacks

As I have gotten older and lived a little bit of life, there are two insights I've gained about setbacks. The first is when I was younger, setbacks upset me much more than they do now. In fact, the younger I was the more setbacks bothered me, and the older I have become the less they bother me. I think the reason why is because I know God does great comebacks.

The second insight is that the less successful I was the more setbacks bothered me, and the more success I've had the less setbacks bother me. The more success you have, the more you understand there is much more success out there for you. The less success you have, especially when you're just starting out or just trying to break through, it bothers you a lot more. Some of the setbacks I had earlier in my life in my ministry and my career were upsetting to me— very upsetting. The setbacks still bother me, but I now have a better perspective, which is found in 1 Corinthians 2:9:

> *But, it is just as the scriptures say. What God has planned for people who love him is more than eyes have seen or ears have heard. It has never even entered our minds.*

Memorize that Scripture. Reflect or meditate on it. God has marvelous plans for you, and they're greater than your mind can conceive. I love that Scripture because I can dream up some pretty good stuff, and the Bible says God has plans even greater than we can dream ourselves.

Drop the Setback Mentality

God wants you to have a life-changing comeback, but there are specific steps you must take.

The first step is you must drop the *setback mentality*, a phrase coined by my long-time friend, Tim Storey, who has coached many people, including celebrities, into comebacks. I think setback mentality is a good description of what can happen to a person who has a setback.

What is a setback mentality? A setback mentality is when you're self-absorbed. You are preoccupied with your setback and the problems it has created. That preoccupation keeps you from moving forward into your comeback. You must get rid of the setback mentality, as it will have you thinking that everyone else—and this is really important—is somehow aware of your setback.

People who have a setback mentality think that everyone else sees them as a failure. Of course, that is not what everyone thinks; in fact, it is what very few people think. And those few people who do you should not acknowledge. Once you have your comeback, those people will be the biggest haters. So lose the setback mentality. Do not allow yourself to keep playing the setback over and over in your mind.

Have you ever noticed how certain companies or teams have remarkable comebacks or turnarounds, and it appears that nothing has changed except there is a new coach or CEO? Oftentimes very little may appear to have changed, but the mentality changed. Someone came into the situation and said, "We can have a comeback. We can turn this thing around." The setback mentality is dropped and replaced by a comeback mentality.

In order to drop the setback mentality, you must realize that setbacks are temporary and that they don't define you. You must remember the things you have achieved. You may need to take time today to think about what you have achieved and the obstacles you have overcome. Instead of focusing on the setback, focus on your accomplishments. Get out your resume and look at all you have done. Look at your awards, look at your degree, look at your certificates. Realize what you have accomplished in your life in many different areas. Help yourself realize that one setback, or even a series of setbacks, does not cancel your achievements and accomplishments. It's amazing how this will affect your mentality. You can't allow the setback mentality, that negative thinking, to get inside of you, because it will keep you from taking the steps toward your comeback.

God is in the redemption business, the restoration business, the reconciliation business. When you link yourself with God, when you allow Jesus Christ to come into your life and the power of the Holy Spirit to work through you, it is amazing what you can do. The first step toward a comeback happens when you leave the setback mentality behind.

Exit Survival Mode

You have to take another step: exit survival mode. Some have been in survival mode for far too long.

I had lunch not long ago with someone who has had some incredible setback experiences: a loss of a loved one and a financial setback. As I was talking with this person, he said that last year he kind of just checked out. That phrase "checked out" really hit me. I think that when people check out, they are in survival mode. You may need to be in survival mode for a while to heal, but that can only be a temporary place.

There comes a point when after you've checked out, licked your wounds, and got your bearings, you have to exit survival mode. You can't stay there. You may think you need to stay in that season longer, but it is a dangerous for your comeback. You can get comfortable in survival mode because it can be quite a pity party where you dwell on how you've been wronged, how things are not fair, or how things haven't gone your way. As I said to the person I had lunch with, "It's time to get out of that. It's time for your comeback." That individual agreed that it was time to get out of survival mode and get back in the game. Injuries happen, and when they do you heal, and you play again.

I had a weightlifting accident years ago doing a closed-grip bench press. Usually in a bench press, you hold the bar the width of your shoulders, but if you want to get a certain strength, you put your hands close together. But you don't have the same control when you lift like that, and I did it without anyone spotting me. When I put the bar back up, I heard the clank, indicating the bar was set. Only it had set on one side, not the other. As I was getting off the bench, the bar and all the weight came down on my face, breaking my orbital bone among other injuries. After I healed from that injury, it was not easy going back into the weight room. But I had to overcome that in order to get back to working out.

There comes a point when your comeback must begin, but it can't when you are in survival mode. Survival mode is a fruitless way to live. There is no growth, no progress, and no impact in survival mode. You will never become who God created you to be, nor will you experience the marvelous plans God has for your life as long as you stay in survival mode. God did not put you on this earth just to survive; God put you here to thrive. And God wants you to thrive in the life He has for you; in the gifts, talents, and opportunities he's given you. He wants you to overcome the setback, to break through the obstacles that stand in your way.

Former Army Staff Sergeant Dan Nevins knows about overcoming obstacles and making a comeback. He lost a leg when injured in combat. Six years later, he walks without a hitch in his gait. He skis and has even climbed Mount Kilimanjaro. Nevins finds great joy in walking into a military hospital with his artificial limb under his pants. He will strike up a conversation with soldiers who are learning to deal with an amputation and show them there is nothing they can't do.

Survival mode is a very isolated way of living. The checking out can mean a lot of alone time. Now there is value in a season of reflection and introspection, but you need to reconnect with friends and get back into the swing of life. If you are going to have the comeback God wants for you, you must take the step out of survival mode and into a place of expectation for what God wants to do in your life.

Restart Your Dream Engine

Another step that will lead to your comeback is to restart your dream engine.

I live in NASCAR country; in fact, we have one of their tracks in Richmond. I like going to those races, especially when they announce, "Gentlemen, start your engines," and those engines create an incredible sound you not only hear but feel. When those eight-hundred horsepower cars start driving around the track, it is quite a sound. And when you have had a setback, your dream engine will need to be restarted.

Setbacks do not control your life. *You* control your life. You decide that you are going to dream again. You've had a setback; it happens to the best of us. Peyton Manning, the record-setting quarterback of the Indianapolis Colts, had neck surgery in the off-season, but he never thought he would miss any playing time. Three neck surgeries later, he ended up missing the entire 2011 NFL season. One of the greatest quarterbacks in NFL history, known for his incredible durability, had experienced quite a setback. His setback was intensified when the Colts decided to let him go and draft a new quarterback, Andrew Luck, to take his place. Peyton ended up signing with the Denver Broncos and went on to win his fifth MVP. He twice led the Broncos to the Super Bowl and won it in 2016, retiring from professional football after having a fantastic comeback.

You can decide that you are going to restart your dream engine; that you are not going to allow your dreams to falter and go away. I love seeing dreams fulfilled. I think it is a powerful thing when God works in someone's life in such a way that He begins to fulfill his or her dreams. You've got to ask for God's blessing and help. Many miss out on God's blessings that come only when you ask. Simply put, a blessing is God's supernatural favor, which comes to those who ask for it. There comes a point when you decide to ask for your dreams to be fulfilled and will not allow the setback to define you anymore. You determine to move forward into the dream God has for you.

Joseph was one of the first great dreamers in the Bible. He had an incredible dream, and his own brothers tried to kill him to stop the dream from happening. They were the original haters. They didn't like that their little brother had bigger dreams than they had. There will always be people in your life who try to steal your dreams, who try to distract you from your dreams. There will always be people who will put down your dreams, who will try to discourage you from your comeback. My advice to you as a spiritual leader, a motivational speaker, and someone who has seen many dreams come true is: *do not listen to those people!*

When you are young you have dreams, and occasionally older adults, because of their own disappointments and setbacks, will try to talk you out of them and make you lower your expectations. But do not allow that to happen. Even well-meaning people who care about you and have more life experience may attempt to dissuade you.

Many times the one thing that older, more experienced people will tell younger people is that the finances will not be there. But I want you to know that it is amazing how God provides. So don't let anyone tell you that finances should hold you back from your dream. I have experienced how God provides finances in both my personal life and my ministry. Many of my dreams have been fulfilled as God both guided and provided. If you really believe God has given you this dream and is leading you, you should move in that direction. Remember, God is pro-vision.

The question for you should be, "What is next? Not what's happened, but what is next?" What does your comeback look like to you? It may be launching a new project. It may be trying a new approach. Take direct, specific action in movement toward your dream. You've had setbacks. You've learned from them. You're ready for the comeback. You understand the components of that comeback. Now it is time to start taking the steps. It is not enough to have information. It is time to act. Act from the information and knowledge you now have. God has a great comeback in store for you!

RELATIONAL 7 COMEBACK

You may be divorced, estranged from a family member, or no longer have a good friend. You have experienced a relational setback. The pain these setbacks can bring to your life is intense. A study has recently come out from two researchers, Ethan Cross of the University of Michigan and Edward Smith of Columbia University. They discovered pain of rejection is more than just a figure of speech. The regions of the brain responding to physical pain actually overlap with those responding to social rejection. Using brain imaging, they were able to determine not just physical pain but emotional pain affects us in a similar way.

They put subjects into four situations and measured their response in the brain using magnetic resonance imaging. One was when they viewed a photo of their former boyfriend or girlfriend and thought about that breakup. Another was when they viewed a photo of a friend and thought positively about their friendship. A third was when a device that produced a gentle, comforting warmth was placed on their arm. And the final one was when a device that was hot enough to cause some physical pain, though not physical damage, was placed on their arm. The two negative situations caused a response in the brain that was identical; they overlapped in regards to actual physical pain and the pain of social rejection. So it turns out relational rejection really is painful. Our brains communicate to us the pain of rejection.

You may have had such an experience. You have had a relational setback of some type. It is understandable then you might be fearful of rejection, not wanting to experience that pain again. Relational rejection is really about who you are. It is about your personhood. It's not about your performance, it's about your personhood. This type of rejection is a setback for any of us.

However, friendships are absolutely crucial for our lives. It is in relationships that we receive the necessary support and encouragement any person needs. I had breakfast recently with one of my longtime friends, a thirty-year friend who was in town visiting from California. It is always great to get together with old friends and people you've known for a long time. He is presently single, and we were talking about his single life and the single experience at this point in his life. One of the things that he said that struck me was, "I'm really not lonely." I said, "Well, that's great. How do you keep from being lonely?" He said, "Well, I just have a lot of relationships. I have a lot of friendships. I have a lot of partnerships. And they provide me the kind of support and encouragement that I need even though I don't have a spouse."

Relationships have to be built on a foundation of openness and trust. You need to have openness. There must be trust in order for relationships to work. Relationships are crucial, but you are afraid of rejection. So how do you have a relationship comeback?

Keep fear from preventing friendship. Fear of rejection causes you to lose out on the necessary and needed relationships you need to be fulfilled and happy. You can't have friendship if you fear rejection, because your fear of rejection will keep you from starting new relationships.

Community Is Crucial

A Christian perspective, a biblical perspective of relationships is they constitute normative Christianity. Christianity creates community. Community is not unique solely to Christianity, but it is a term that best describes the Church. The Bible calls the Church the family of God. The Bible describes the Church as the body of Christ. God has designed life that we might be joined together in relationship. He doesn't want us to go it alone.

When people say, "I am a Christian or I'm a follower of Christ, but I don't go to church," it makes no sense. It is impossible to be a follower of Christ and not be in the family of God where all the followers gather together. It is not normative, it is not healthy. God wants His people to be in relationship.

Some people do not want to be part of organized religion. But organized religion and a local church are not the same. Part of why the church I pastor has been so successful, effective, and appealing is because it is not traditional or religious. People find they can come and be a part of it without having to get their act together first, dress a certain way, or know the lingo or liturgy in order to be part of the church.

I understand very well having worked with people for many years people have bad church experiences. They feel they've been judged by other people, they feel they've been unloved and uncared for, they feel powerless against leadership. So they keep their distance from the church because people judge you, hurt you, mistreat you and don't love unconditionally. Some of those may be true, but the answer is creating boundaries, not leaving all relationships. Over twenty years ago, John Townsend and Henry Cloud wrote the book, *Boundaries*. They helped many to understand healthy boundaries, learn to say no, and have better relationships. A few years ago, John Townsend came out with a new book, *Beyond Boundaries*. Townsend writes about how healthy it is to establish boundaries, but your boundaries should not keep you from ever entering into new and better relationships. Opening up to new relationships is crucial. There is no other way to have a relationship comeback.

Criteria for a New Relationship

What are the criteria for a new relationship? People have to be healthy and safe. You don't just open yourself up to anyone, but the opposite response of opening yourself up to no one is not a healthy response either. This is not the way God designed you to live. You can never have enough friends. New friendships even as you grow older are extremely valuable and can bring new information, new experiences, and new adventures you would not have had without them.

Sometimes we withdraw for good reasons. I can tell you I've done it. As someone who works with people for a living, I have withdrawn from people because they are not healthy or safe. They hurt, they cause trouble, and they need to be avoided. But when you withdraw from certain people for good reason, you still need to reenter relational life. You must open yourself up to new people and new relationships that could bring such joy and happiness into your life.

Don't let your fear of rejection keep you from new friendships and new opportunities to experience what you've never experienced before. New people may run in a different group, a different crowd, do things in a different way, and they open you up to new experiences. I'm referring to good experiences, not bad stuff, sinful practices, and unhealthy behaviors.

There is always a risk of being hurt when you open yourself up, but it can be a measured risk. You can calculate your risk by observing different people and seeing whether they fit into the healthy category or the good people category. And if they do, then begin your comeback. I believe the best place—not the only place, but the best place—would be a church. I'm not declaring everyone in a church is healthy or good, but the majority of people are. The church provides you a built-in opportunity for relationship and you should take advantage of it.

Deal with Conflict

Many relational setbacks are the result of conflict. You did not deal with conflict in a healthy way. Who doesn't have conflict in their relationships? Conflict isn't necessarily bad—it can lead to a better relationship—but it can also lead to the end of a relationship. You can strengthen your relationship by dealing with conflict. Don't run from strife, address it. How you address it makes all the difference in the world. Listening is your number one strategy for addressing conflict. Listening, not talking, not airing your grievance—listening is how to solve conflict.

You'll never resolve a conflict unless both sides are willing to listen to the other. When people are able to listen to each other's points of view even if they don't agree, maybe they can come to a place of agreement or at least agree to disagree rather than being disagreeable. Can you listen? Can you resolve conflicts that will inevitably come up in any relationship? In relationships you have to choose your battles. Major on the majors. Much in life can really just be overlooked if we come right down to it, unless you really want to fight all the time and risk ending the friendship. You may have strong opinions. I have strong opinions, so I understand. But I have come to a place in my life where I don't want unnecessary conflict. I don't want arguments to risk ending friendships. There may be a time where I can't bend on a particular issue or principle, but it will be a minority of the time. Whether it is social issues, leadership issues or family issues, before you throw down ask yourself if it is worth it.

In relationships, don't dwell on the downers. Downers are those things that are negative. There is plenty of negativity in this world. Stuff will come into your friendships, your relationships, your family life; just move past it to the more positive. Dwelling does not strengthen relationships, it ends up straining them. You don't want to be a part of bringing increased strain into a relationship and possibly causing it to end.

You listen, you respond to what you hear, and you try to make things better if you can. I'm not claiming it always can be done. Even if you can't always get to a place where everyone is happy, if people know they've been heard they feel better. People have a need to confide, and they have a need to be heard. When they feel that that has happened, it strengthens any relationship.

Being a God-Pleaser, Not a People-Pleaser

To truly have a relationship comeback requires you to be a God-pleaser more than a people-pleaser. It may sound counterintuitive, but it is true. If you seek to please people more than God, you actually end up with unhealthy relationships. Galatians1:10 tells us, "I'm not trying to please people. I want to please God. Do you think I'm trying to please people? If I were doing that, I would not be a servant of Christ." Our focus is on being a God-pleaser, not a people pleaser.

Why does trying to please people not work? You can never please everyone. Accepting you can't make everyone happy helps your relationships, it doesn't harm them. Some are driven to be liked, to want everyone to be happy, to have everyone to get along. It may be great in theory, but in reality everyone can't always get along. People are never always going to agree. Two people can be in the same situation and see it in two totally different ways.

People-pleasing ultimately leads you to unhappiness. When your life is about pleasing other people who will never be fully satisfied, you'll just be frustrated and you'll be unhappy. Our desire is not pleasing people, it's pleasing God. When we want to please people we begin to conform our lifestyle because we fear rejection.

I had an interesting experience at the golf course recently. I decided at the last minute to go play, and I really hadn't planned it for the week. I showed up as what they call a single—I didn't have a partner or group to play with. They put me in a group with these three young guys. They were talking in ways different than people usually talk around me, talking about subjects they usually don't talk about and consuming a fair amount of beer in the process. One of them actually hit me with a golf ball! The more I listened to these guys talk, I could just see the pressure to conform. The loudest guy in the group asked me if I wanted a beer, and when I told him no he kept pressuring me to have one. The more I listened, the more I thought how strong the pressure is to please people—do what they are doing, talk like they are talking, and not be different. I wanted so much to tell them who I was, but I kept it a secret the whole time because it really was a lot more fun.

If you are a people-pleaser, you are going to conform your lifestyle to what pleases people and you are not going to please God. Paul said: "If I were doing that, I wouldn't be a servant of Christ." If you are going to follow Christ, if you are going to be His servant, then you need to conform your lifestyle according to the teachings of Jesus.

When you are a people pleaser you stunt your spiritual growth. You don't grow and develop. You can't expand or deepen your walk with God because you more concerned about what other people think. As long as you are more concerned about what others think than about what God thinks there is no possibility of a comeback. The concern about rejection ends up being very unhealthy. We conform to others' opinions and are less happy.

Romans 12:2 says, "Do not conform to the pattern of this world, but be transformed by the renewing of your mind." The renewing of your mind means the more you read and study the Bible, the more your mind gets cleaned up, straightened out, and thinks straight. You become healthier as you are transformed. The principles, teachings, and commands of the Bible are complete truth. The more you learn them and apply them in your life, the more pleasing you are to God. Your mind begins a total transformation, where how you think and speak is changed. You become more like Christ and your actions change because your mind has been transformed. By focusing on what God wants for your life, you please God rather than pleasing people.

Being a God-pleaser and not a people-pleaser does not mean you go around ticking people off and being a jerk. You can't act whatever way you like and then claim you are just pleasing God, not people. Pleasing God doesn't mean you will make everybody else mad. Pleasing God doesn't mean you will be the last person anyone wants to be around. If you live out the preeminent teaching of Jesus, you love your neighbor as yourself. Followers of Jesus are people who believe in loving others. When we follow Jesus, we want to please Him and we are going to do many loving, caring things people will like. You don't say, "I'm a God pleaser and I don't care what anyone thinks!"

As you endeavor to please God, many people will be blessed. But if you have to choose between God or people, you choose God. You choose His ways. You choose His plan for your life. The only one you need to be concerned about pleasing is Jesus. If you do, your relationships will be enriched. You will understand how fearing rejection causes you to conform and brings you down paths you don't want to go, becoming a person you don't want to be.

God Accepts You

To properly understand rejection at its most basic level, you need to discern this: God's complete acceptance of you. Too many don't believe it. Maybe for the first time, maybe for the final time, comprehend this salient truth: God accepts you. He may not approve of your behavior, but He accepts you completely. You do not have to first get your act together to come to Jesus. You come to Jesus and then Jesus helps you to get your act together. You don't clean yourself up first then come to Him. You just come as you are. You don't have to get yourself straightened out first. God will help you get straightened out. God will forgive you, He will restore you and He will never reject you.

God sees in you what other people many times don't see: your value and your potential. When I think about our loving heavenly Father, I try in my finite fatherly way to consider how I think about my own kids. What do I think about them? A loving father should believe in his children's potential. I have always believed in my sons' potential and encouraged them in any way I can. Even now as young men with their whole lives ahead of them, I believe in their potential and do my best to show them that they are exceptional to me. I'm just a father trying to do that with my kids. Imagine our perfect heavenly Father—how much He loves you, how much He believes in you, how much He sees what you can become.

People will never be able to fully see you that way, even the people who love you the most. They will never be able to see you the way God sees you. And they will never be able to love you as much as God does. It is crucial for your own personhood and for your relationships to know no one— not a husband, not a wife, not a mother, not a father, not a best friend—can love you fully the way you need to be loved except God. You need God in your life. You need to have a relationship with God so you can ground yourself in His unconditional love and acceptance of you. Then you can develop relationships with other people that will be healthy, relationships that will be good, though never perfect.

God accepts you. God loves you unconditionally, which is hard to understand because everyone else loves conditionally. Even when we try our best, it is simply beyond our human ability to be unconditional in our love. We are flawed. We are not perfect. But God is perfect. God loves us in a unique way. And that love then gives us freedom to become who God created us to be. Freedom you cannot experience if you are constantly concerned about what others think of you and whether they will accept you or reject you.

When you are free you know God accepts you, God loves you, God has a plan for your life. God wants to direct you to a place of realizing your full potential. It causes you to reach out to others and form healthy relationships. To love God and be loved by God does not mean we soak in all of the love in a selfish way and keep it to ourselves—rather, having received this knowledge of God's love and acceptance of us, we can then love other people. We can accept other people. We can endeavor to love them the way that God loves us.

This is the essence of the Christian faith. And why so many people choose to enter into relationship with God through Jesus Christ. This is such a healthy way to live, establishing a right approach to relationships. The best way to be in healthy relationships is to know God's acceptance of you, to receive His love for you, and then share that love with other people. When God's love comes in your life, it frees you to be a loving person. And it is amazing how love begets love, how forgiveness begets forgiveness, and how grace begets grace.

Have you accepted Jesus knowing that He has accepted you? If you will just take a step toward God, God won't meet you halfway, He will come to you. He will welcome you to begin to live your life the way that God intended it to be. Just ask Him to forgive you of all your past sins, mistakes, and failures. Thank Him for His unconditional love and acceptance of you. Ask Him to help you to realize your full potential believing He will guide and direct you in a way you can share His love with others. When you do this, you are well on your way to a powerful comeback.

FINANCIAL 8 COMEBACK

Financial setbacks happen to all of us. One bad investment decision, one hospital stay, or one spending spree and we are in need of a financial comeback. Of course there are many more setbacks that can impact us financially, and sometimes we are hit with several of them all at once. There are times when nothing could have been done to stop a financial hit from impacting our lives. When this happens, we need to ask God for help.

Over twenty times in the New Testament it says this: *ask!* Jesus said, "You have not because you ask not." If you try to do it on your own, that doesn't work and then you are still in your setback. You have no one but yourself to blame because you never asked God for help. Jesus said this as well, "Don't worry about what you will eat and drink and what you will wear! Only people who don't know God are always worrying about these things. Your father knows what you need." (Matthew 6:31–32)

Let God know you are nervous and fearful. Tell Him you don't know where the money is going to come from. Ask Him to bless you, to bring in resources from places that you don't even know about. I've been asking God for a lot of things for a long time and God comes through time and time again. I started our church from scratch with twenty people and $2000. We have had many setbacks along the way but God has always provided. James 4:2 says, "You want something you don't have? You'll do anything to get it. You'll even kill but you still can't get what you want. You won't get it by fighting and arguing. You should pray for it." Instead of trying to scheme, manipulate, and work your network, ask God. Pray and your heavenly Father will help you.

How can it hurt to ask? Why would you not ask? Some think they don't want to bother God. He isn't like us—we get bothered, He doesn't get bothered. God is so big. He's so gigantic. It is hard for our human mind try to understand the infinite nature of God. If God tells us to ask, we should ask. God is concerned about everything that you are concerned about. God knows all about you. He loves you. He wants to help you. Just ask for help.

We all need money to live, and when we have a setback we need money even more. We need to trust God will not leave us in financial need rather than making money our master. Money is fascinating on many levels. I recently read about our actual bills in the US currency. I thought it interesting that our money used to be made out of silk. Then it was made out of linen, then it went to cotton, and it's now a combination of cotton and paper. The number of times that you can fold a bill before it will ultimately rip is 4,000 times. It costs 4.2 cents to actually make a bill. So it takes a little bit of money to make money. A dollar bill only makes it about 18 months before it's taken out of circulation because it's too worn out, but a $50 or a $100 bill lasts nine years. Nine years versus a year and a half. The difference is the amount of use that those different kinds of bills get.

Sound Money Management

There are other times, probably the majority of the time, when our decisions have created a financial setback. Actions we have taken bring us to a place where we need a comeback. To make a financial setback, you have to practice sound money management. The way to get to a place where you are comfortable with your financial situation, you have financial security or financial freedom, is all about money management. It is not about how much money you make but how you manage whatever money you make. Every once in a while I'll read a story about the librarian or the teacher or the custodian who at the end of his or her life gives a giant gift to a school or another worthy organization. Many are amazed someone on that income could ever get to a place where they give away this much money. The only explanation is sound financial management.

You manage your money or your money will manage you. Either you're going to handle money well or not. If you don't handle it well, then it's going to end up managing you. This is what happens to too many that leads to a financial setback. Money is a wonderful servant but a horrible master. You want money to serve you. You do not want to serve money. If you are serving money right now, you know how miserable it is. There is nothing worse than the pounding pressure of bill collectors and all kinds of pressure about finances. It is a miserable place to be. The only way to have a comeback is to get a handle on your finances.

Hebrews 13:5 says, "Don't fall in love with money. Be satisfied with what you have. The Lord has promised that He will not leave us or desert us." I think the Bible gives us some excellent advice when it says don't fall in love with money and be satisfied with what you have. The world, as a whole, has fallen in love with money. Materialism grips our Western culture. It causes us to think more money brings happiness, and with more money problems would disappear. But that is not true. The stories of some people who have won the lottery are incredible and how their lives get so messed up after they get money. There are stories of athletes who had fantastic multimillion-dollar contracts and then don't even have enough money to live on when they retire from sports. These are very young men who cannot live comfortably because of poor money management.

Learn To Be Satisfied

We have to learn to be satisfied with what we have. This is learned behavior; it is not natural to us. Learning to be satisfied means not buying on impulse—not just buying something because we see it and think we need it or want it. It means not buying out of emotion just to give us a temporary emotional boost. Thinking a new set of golf clubs or a new pair of shoes will make you happy is a fallacy. The feeling will go away and you will still be in your setback.

Financial comebacks happen when you pray for it before you pay for it. I can't tell you how many times in making financial decisions before I've paid for it I've prayed for it. In praying for it, a number of things have happened: I've gotten a better deal or I've come to realize it wasn't a good idea, so I didn't pay for it. It is amazing how God can show us insights and reveal to us wisdom if we pray first. Right now my wife and I are considering a major purchase. She is in favor of it and I have not decided whether I am in favor of it. So I will pray about it. I'm taking a trip for a couple of days, which always gives me a little chance to think while I'm traveling. I'm going to be thinking and praying about it a little bit more before I decide. But whatever decision I come to, I want to pray for it first.

Not every financial decision may need to be prayed about. You may not pray before you go to the grocery store but you need to pray before you go to the car dealer. You need to pray before you go to the realtor. You need to pray before you make significant purchases. It is important to ask if this is what God wants for you. I don't know if God wants a particular kind of car for you but I believe God will lead you to the best deal for that car. Sometimes you walk away from a purchase because God has something better for you. I know every time I made those kinds of decisions they have been good decisions. I'm a proponent of a dollar saved is a dollar earned. Why pay full price for something when you can get it at a discount? I think it's just wise money management.

When you have to have it now, then you pay full price. This leaves you with less money. Repeating this same behavior over and over is how financial setbacks happen. If you get something for 50 percent off, it's like getting two items for the price of one. What could your financial situation look like if you just stop paying full price for everything and look to get the best deal? Not just look for a deal but pray for a deal.

Spend Wisely

Be wise in how you spend your money. Don't overbuy. Don't be envious of others. Be diligent with your finances. It is challenging but if you want a financial comeback, you've got to get your expenses in line with your income. There's no way to get around that basic reality. You have to live by a budget. If you don't know what's going out and what's coming in, then you have a setback. One crucial practice in making financial decisions is: always sleep on it. Salespeople want you to make the decision now. Taking the time to think and pray will benefit you greatly. This principle works in all decisions. I tell my staff, my family, and anyone who presses for me for a decision the same thing: "If you have to have an answer now, then it is no." If I sleep on it, the answer may be yes. But if you have to know now, the answer is no. Sleeping on a decision could save you a lot of financial setbacks.

One step you can take to jumpstart your financial comeback is a thirty-day spending fast. If you've never heard of this, it simply means cutting all nonessential spending. The essential spending are your bills—everything else is cut. You don't go to the grocery store and only eat what is already in the house. You don't eat out at any restaurants for the whole month. You don't buy gas, you get rides. No entertainment, no clothes shopping, no spending except on pre-committed bills. If you really want to start your comeback, this will give you a little extra money and a little more sense of security. It is just like the spiritual principle of fasting. Fasting shows you how big a deal food is in your life. And when you take the food away, it's a revealing experience. What it would be like to take your family through this thirty-day spending fast just to help them appreciate and understand how much money is spent each month.

Get Out of Debt

Sound money management that leads to a comeback must address the debt issue. How do you approach indebtedness? Do you just think it is just part of life? Paying someone else interest is not the way to a comeback. Having someone pay you interest on your investments is the way to go. Most people think a mortgage is an acceptable debt. But how long is the mortgage? Get out your statement and look at how much goes on the principal and how much goes on to interest. Years ago I looked at it and I couldn't accept having a thirty-year mortgage. I got down to a ten-year mortgage. You can be excited to open your bill when you see how much principal is paid versus how much interest is paid. It completely flips to your advantage. The most significant debt for most people is credit cards. The interest rates are far higher than a mortgage, double or even triple the amount. It's a lot of money to be paying every month. And it is unsecured debt. At least your house has value.

How do you get rid of debt? There is no magic formula; it is a matter of discipline. You must decide there can be no comeback unless the debt is gone. Experts disagree on the best approach. Some say pay the smallest debt off first because you'll get good feedback. You'll feel good about paying it off and now you can tackle the next debt. Some experts say pay the debt that has the highest interest. Then work to the next highest until all debt is gone. I don't know which is best for you, but I do know this— get rid of the debt.

When you're debt-free, all the pressure that goes with indebtedness will be gone. It will give you an incredible amount of freedom. But even better, that money can then be invested—turning your whole financial picture around. Instead of paying someone else interest, you now get paid interest. This is an unbelievable turnaround in any person's financial situation. Instead of paying others to use their money, people start paying you to use your money. When you're in a place where you really feel good about your financial situation, where you're practicing sound money management, you are well on your way to a financial comeback.

80/10/10 Formula

I think the 80/10/10 formula is the way to structure your finances. The formula is this: live on 80 percent, give God 10 percent, and save 10 percent of your income. There is no way you'll have a significant setback if you practice this simple formula. Live on 80 percent (on a budget). Give God His 10 percent (the tithe), then you're not robbing God and the blessing of God will be upon your life. Save 10 percent so you'll always have money in the bank. It's a marvelous way to live. One of my college professors taught me this when I was an undergraduate years ago. I made that a goal and it took some time to achieve, but it has been a marvelous way to structure my finances. You may have to create systems to help you do it like automatic savings, where the deduction is taken out of your checking account and put into a mutual fund. A similar automatic deduction can come out of your checking account and into your church's account so you faithfully tithe each month. Too many wait to see how much money is left over at the end of the month and seemingly never have any money left over. It's amazing how you can live fine on the rest of the money, but when you didn't have the automatic money being taken out, you just ended up spending it.

This is how you have a financial comeback. You save money. You get out of debt. You don't overspend. You live within your means. You become financially free and financially secure. You've got to have a plan. You've got to put these principles into practice in your life. If you work them long enough, you'll get out of the setback and into the comeback.

Be a Generous Giver

A complete financial comeback can only happen with the blessing of God. You need God's favor, and that only happens when you are a generous giver. Malachi 3:8 says, "You people are robbing me. And you are asking, 'How are we robbing you, God?' You are robbing me off the offerings and the ten percent that belongs to me." It is never a wise financial strategy to rip off God. Think about it. Who would be so crazy as to steal from God? You should not steal from anybody, and definitely not God! And people do it all the time. Verse 10 says, "I challenge you to put me to the test. You bring the entire ten percent so there will be food in my house and I'll open up the windows of heaven and flood you with blessing after blessing." You can't make it financially, you can't have security, you can't expect a comeback if you rob God and steal from him. It's just that simple.

In Luke 6:38, Jesus says, "If you give to others, you will be given a full amount in return. It will be packed down, shaken together, and spilling over." You can't outgive God. As long as you are generous, God will always respond to that generosity. A scarcity mentality thinks the pie is only so big and you have to protect your piece. God wants you to have an abundance mentality. God can make the pie immeasurably large. Don't put limits on God's generosity. If you want to live with the blessings of God, you have to be a giver. Acts 20:35 tells us, "Remember that our Lord Jesus said, 'More blessings come from giving than from receiving.'" You have to be a generous giver. The happy people are the giving people. People who are generous are the people who really find happiness with money because everyone knows how good it feels to give.

Why is Christmas the number one holiday? It may be family, but more people come to Thanksgiving than Christmas. It's the gift-giving. People like to get gifts, and they like to give them as well. It makes you feel good to give. It's so funny when young parents are getting ready for Christmas. The kid doesn't even know what half the presents are, but it doesn't matter. The new parents just love to show their love by giving. I love to give. It makes me feel good. It breaks the grip of materialism in my life. It puts my heart where it needs to be. I love the response people have to giving. Recently we celebrated my mother-in-law's eightieth birthday at a beautiful banquet. That morning all of her seven children and their spouses gathered together for breakfast. I bought everyone breakfast that day, and it made me happy to be able to do it. Generosity ensures a comeback.

Generosity rises out of contentment. We come to a place where we learn to be contented. It's hard to be generous when you're not content. True generosity is not an occasional event. It comes from having a big heart. We are to be the kind of person who wants to give. If we wait till we can "afford" to give, we never will. If that's how we're going to look at giving, then there will be no generosity. The same concept applies to having children. We'll wait to have kids until we can afford it. Well, you'll be waiting a long time. You have kids even if you can't afford them and you go from there. Amazingly God provides and you're able to buy them what they need.

To be generous really takes courage to change from being a receiver to a giver. But it can happen, and that change propels your comeback. So many people are not content, they're not financially free because they're mismanaging their money, and they aren't generous. They give the birthday gift, buy the Christmas gift, and give something for the anniversary. That is not a giving, generous person. That is just someone who is just fulfilling society's obligations at a minimum level of giving.

If you're a follower of Jesus Christ, you cannot separate followership from finances. Jesus said you can't serve God and money. Money and God are interconnected. God knows you can't serve Him and money. You've got to come to a place of putting God first. Deuteronomy 14:22–23 says, "The purpose of tithing is to teach you to learn to always put God first in your life." Tithing helps you learn how to put God first. God uses tithing and other forms of generosity to establish that He is first. When you put God first, you don't worry about money because you trust that God will provide for you. God will keep blessing you and taking care of you. And your giving is storing up treasure in heaven.

The blessing of God is absolutely tied to your level of generosity. There is no doubt that receiving God's blessings makes you happy. There is no doubt that blessings create a comeback. God orchestrates events in such a marvelous way. You could plan, you could push, and you could try to make it happen yourself or you could just be generous, put God first in your life, and watch God bless and make things happen for you. That is how you end up moving from a financial setback to a marvelous comeback.

CAREER COMEBACK

Losing your job is a significant setback. Missing out on a promotion or being passed over for a raise is a setback. Many have these unfortunate experiences at some point in their lives maybe even you. Your job, your career is hugely significant in providing for your needs and giving you a sense of purpose. The **US Bureau of Labor** reports by the time you are forty years old, you will have held 10½ jobs. I'm not actually sure what holding half a job is. I think it might have something to do with averages. If you go back and think from the time you were eighteen until the time you are forty, it's amazing how many different jobs you can have. But changing a job and losing your job are two entirely different experiences.

Losing a job can result from many different reasons. You can be laid off, downsized, or fired. The loss of your job can be entirely your fault, partly your fault, or not your fault at all. In the end, regardless of the circumstances, you have lost your livelihood and you need a career comeback. The biggest chunk of your time each day is spent working. Work has a purpose. God is not punishing us by making us work. Genesis 2:15 says, "The Lord God took the man and put

him in the Garden of Eden to work it and to take care of it."
Sin did not enter the world until the Fall in Genesis 3. God's
original purpose was for us to work and enjoy it.

God had a plan from the beginning that we would be
workers. Work reveals our partnership with God. God is in
partnership with us, and the purpose of that partnership is
God wants to get things done and He uses us to do it. God
is a worker, and He has given you an opportunity to be a
worker—and together do something God wants done. We
help God carry out His plan and purpose for this world. He
has multiple plans and multiple purposes to accomplish all
around the world. The grocer supplies the food. The lawyer
brings justice. The homemaker nurtures the children. God
is using all kinds of people in all kinds of ways. And it's
good to be in partnership with God at whatever place or in
whatever role you find yourself.

Jesus says in John 5:17, "My father is always at his
work to this very day and I too, am working." God is
working. Jesus was working when he was on this earth,
partnering with the Father to accomplish His will. Work
is what we do. Workers are who we are. It's not a curse.
It's not a bad deal. Work is not some kind of cruel master
we have to serve. It's what God created us to do. It's not
all that we're to do, it's not all we are, but it does reveal
our partnership with God and what it is God wants to
accomplish in this world. Whatever your job, you may never
know how it ends up impacting other people's lives in a
positive way.

Losing your job is a big emotional blow. The loss of
purpose, the loss of routine, and the loss of income can be
devastating. And there is the loss of friends. Many of our
closest friendships are made at work, and when we no
longer have a job, we can lose those friendships as well.
Like all setbacks it can take some time to recover from the
blow, but your comeback cannot begin until you regain
some emotional footing. Once that happens, your goal is to
make sure you are so indispensable you will never lose your
job again.

Commit to Hard Work

One way to guarantee your career comeback is commit to hard work. Proverbs 12:24 tells us, "Work hard and you will be a leader, be lazy and you will end up a slave." Verse 27 says, "Anyone too lazy to cook will starve but a hard worker is a valuable treasure." Ninety-three CEOs were asked about what makes someone a successful leader. They identified a variety of qualities including vision, character, and people skills. But there was only one quality all CEO's agreed on and it was hard work. The one factor every single CEO said was crucial to successful leadership was hard work.

Look at those who've been successful in the sports world we generally think are so blessed with God-given talent. But there is more to the story. In basketball, Michael Jordan, who many consider the greatest basketball player who ever lived, was legendary for his work ethic especially in the off-season. Wayne Gretzky, considered by many the greatest hockey player of all time, was known for how hard he would practice. Jerry Rice, statistically the greatest wide receiver ever to play professional football, had his workouts emulated by other players because they were so hard and difficult. The greatest players were the hardest workers.

Malcolm Gladwell, the famous author of five bestsellers, wrote the book, *Outliers*, where he expounded on the "10,000-Hour Rule," claiming the key to achieving world-class expertise in any skill is a matter of practicing the correct way for a total of around 10,000 hours. He references a study by Anders Ericsson and asserts that greatness requires an enormous amount of work, using The Beatles' musical talents and Bill Gates' computer savvy as examples. The Beatles performed in Germany over 1,200 times between 1960 and 1964, amassing more than 10,000 hours of playing time. Gates gained access to a high school computer in 1968 at the age of thirteen and spent 10,000 hours programming on it. Becoming the most famous rock band of all time or the richest man in the world mean putting in the work. There are no overnight sensations it is a matter of hard work invested over time that ultimately results in a career comeback.

Self-Discipline Is Required

The indispensable requirement for hard work is self-discipline. You simply have to discipline yourself to do the work. It will always be easier to just binge-watch TV than get up off the couch and do the work. It will always be more enticing to respond to your friends' phone calls and go out. It will always be more fun to surf the web and waste hours at a time. This will never change. It will always be easier to sleep in, goof off and make excuses than to put in the work.

If you keep at it, you will have a comeback. If you keep working, you'll see the results of your hard work. Too many people view hard work as extra work that is too difficult to do. When you work hard, you set yourself apart. You set yourself apart from other people, and this is where you safeguard yourself from another career setback. The difference in your work gets noticed, and that grants you the ability to have influence, to have a position of leadership, and hopefully to positively impact others. This all comes from good old-fashioned hard work—there is just no other way around it. It comes from just disciplining yourself to do what it is you need to do. The results of hard work are a place of leadership and influence, just as Proverbs teaches. Hard work makes you valuable as Proverbs says as well. A hard worker is a valuable treasure to any company, to any organization, to any group. Anyone who works hard will perpetually be of value. If you work hard, you will always find that you're wanted. You will consistently find people will want you because they know you will put in the work. They know you will do the job. And then you will never be without a job, a promotion or a raise.

Hard work means finishing what you start without reminders. Finish what you start without having to be reminded by your boss, by your teacher, or by your coach.

Finish what you start. No one should need to come behind you and remind you to do it—just get it done. Hard work means no excuses. It may be hard and there will be obstacles, but that is life. Hard work means demonstrating initiative and following through. It's one thing to have a great idea, it's another thing to bring that idea into reality. Those are two very different things. At some point ideas have to become reality, and that is spelled *hard work*. There's no other way around it. Everyone has dreams. Why are so few fulfilled? Hard work. There will always be a place on any team, there will always be a place in any company, and there will always be a place with any group for a hardworking person. That person will always find a spot because they're valuable. A hard worker is a valuable treasure, and hard work makes you successful.

Zig Ziglar said, "The elevator to success is out of order, but the stairs are always open." Your career comeback must involve hard work. Set yourself apart from others with your work ethic. You want to be successful in school? Hard work. You're frustrated because you're sitting on the bench and you want to be on the field? Hard work. The bestseller *The Millionaire Next Door* is a book about all these people who are millionaires living in very average homes and driving average cars and yet they have millions of dollars. There are many principles in the book for any person who wants financial security, including living within your means, staying out of debt, consistently investing, and many more financial strategies. What struck me was their belief about hard work. Eighty-five percent of these millionaires believed they weren't smarter or better educated—they simply worked harder.

Commitment to Excellence

Another way to guarantee your career comeback is commit to excellence. "Excellence honors God and inspires people." This is a phrase that I love to champion. It's a phrase I completely believe in. Excellence is something you need to practice in your career to have a comeback. God wants us to excel. God is looking for you to live your life in such a way that you excel at work. Our God is excellent; all He has done, all He has created is excellent. A lack of excellence has all kinds of negative impacts. It may have cost you your job, promotion or raise.

There was a plane crash on September 29, 2006, in the Amazon rainforest in Brazil. It was a crash between a Boeing 737 commercial airliner and an executive jet. When they got the proverbial black box out of the executive jet, what they discovered was the air traffic controllers had told the pilots in the executive jet and the pilots in the Boeing 737 to fly at the same altitude. It was also discovered that the executive jet's transponder was off fifty-four minutes before the time of the crash, the crew only turning it on three minutes before the accident. Footage of the radar screens at the time of the incident revealed the primary radar lost contact with the jet twenty-eight minutes after the transponder was off. The air traffic controller's lack of professional excellence combined with the executive jet's pilot's failure to fly excellently caused 154 people to die.

What is the negative impact of lack of excellence? It could be as horrible as many people losing their lives, or it could be something less than that but still have negative implications in your life. There are all kinds of unnecessary problems created by lack of excellence. We bought a new computer recently for our church and when it came time to install it, they discovered the hard drive was defective. I think if you buy a computer and you take it out of the box, it is supposed to work. How is it something that "drives" the computer gets shipped out of a factory and it does not work? What bothered me most was how we wasted time going back and forth to the store while getting absolutely nothing done at the church because work wasn't done excellently by the computer company.

Whatever you do for a job, whoever you work for, whatever your profession is, ultimately you are not working for your employer or for your customers. You are working for God. God wants you to work in such a way that you excel. Our God is excellent. All He's done, all He's created is excellent. Excellence has implications in so many different areas in your life. Living a life of excellence will enhance your life and career in so many ways. There are certain key principles you can practice and implement that will absolutely power your comeback.

Set High Standards

The first way to be excellent at work is to set high standards. Unless you value excellence, you will never be excellent. If you don't put a value on excellence and quantify it, then you can't define it and you'll never know if you're reaching it. If you're going to achieve excellence, there has to be a standard. We all know there are people, there are companies, there are organizations, and there are teams whose standard is excellence. And time and time and time again they end up hitting that mark. They do so because they have clear standards of what excellence looks like for them. Apple is a great example of consistent excellence. They are one of the highest valued companies in the world with a rabidly loyal customer base because of their excellence.

On the other end of the spectrum are the NFL's Oakland Raiders. The Raiders have as their motto *Commitment to Excellence*. They plaster it on their stadium and in their offices. Have you seen the Oakland Raiders play lately? They're horrible. They're awful! They are nothing close to excellence. As a matter of fact from 2003-2014, they won only 56 games while losing 136 games. They have averaged over eleven losses a year for twelve seasons. You cannot be much worse than that in professional sports. It doesn't mean a thing to say, "We have a commitment to excellence," unless you are actually going to set standards and attain them.

Average is so acceptable in our culture. We live in a world of mediocrity where a lot of people are okay with good enough. Of course you can go that route, but I don't believe that is a godly way to do it. What ought to drive you is the fact God didn't place you on this earth to be mediocre. God hasn't given you your one and only life to strive for average. God wants you to be excellent. Christ followers ought to be the best at whatever they do. The people who claim to follow Christ, those who serve an excellent God, ought to— by their own life and work—exhibit that kind of excellence. Standards have a way of quantifying what success and excellence look like. When you can point to them and understand what they are, then you have excellence.

Work with Enthusiasm

A second excellence principle is to work with enthusiasm. People who are excellent at what they do have enthusiasm. The word "enthusiasm" comes from two words, the word *en* which means "in," and the word *theos* which means "God." So, to be enthusiastic means you're literally "in God." If you're in God, then you should be naturally enthusiastic. You should have an enthusiasm that comes from the reality that ultimately you're working for God, not for man. When you're working for God and you understand the purpose that God has placed you on this earth for, then the work He's given you can be done with enthusiasm.

I am a huge believer in effort. Effort has much to do with enthusiasm. There is an enthusiasm quotient that depends on the person, the situation, and the circumstances. But what is most defining of excellence is the effort that is given. Effort is something all of us control. No one can stop you from being enthusiastic. You can stop yourself, but no one can stop you.

You can have circumstances that are discouraging, you can be around people who certainly make life more challenging, but ultimately it comes down to you and your effort. The Bible says in Colossians 3:23, "Whatever you do, work at it with all your heart." This is the description of enthusiasm in your job. Those who are enthusiastic work with all their heart; they don't work with half their heart. Effort is defined as "wholeheartedness." It is those who give their whole heart to whatever they do.

Maybe you're a student. Your job at this point in your life is to study. You may need a comeback to get into college or graduate school, or go to the school you dream of attending. What does effort look like to a student? It looks like working with all your heart in your studies. It doesn't mean, "I like English, so I work hard in that, but I don't like math so I don't work hard in that." Students need to understand and appreciate that your enthusiasm and effort has to be wholehearted.

What does effort look like in the home? Those of you who are homemakers have a unique challenge, and it has to do with accountability. Only you know whether you're really working up to the standards, only you know if you're really putting forth the best effort. At certain points it can be seen, but in many other areas only you know if you are doing excellent work. But those of you who find yourselves without accountability, you do have accountability to God. You do answer to God for the effort that you put forth in what it is that God has called you to do.

Pay Attention to Detail

Another principle for excellence on the job is to pay attention to detail. Some may say they are not a detail-oriented person by personality and thus are exempt from this principle. But the issue is not whether you're a detail-oriented person. I am a big-picture visionary leader and I very much pay attention to detail. I'm not a detail-oriented person or else I couldn't focus on the larger picture, but I am certainly a person who pays attention to detail. There is a difference between being detail-oriented and making sure proper attention is paid to what is most important.

I like the story about Walt Disney when they were producing the movie *Snow White*. The illustrator spent two hundred forty days working on a four-and-a-half minute segment in which Snow White was playing with the dwarfs while they were making soup and destroying the kitchen. Walt Disney liked the scene because he thought it was funny. But as the film and the project went on, he determined that it just didn't fit with the flow of the picture so he cut it. Two hundred forty days of animation work down the tubes. Disney decided that if the film was going to work, the flow had to be perfect. He had to choose between what is good and what is excellent. Ultimately, he chose what was best and *Snow White* became one of the great animation films of all time.

There are many things that are acceptable and even good. There are far less that are great and even excellent. The difference between acceptable and great, between good and excellent is the little things—the details. You have to pay more attention to the little things. If you are a fan of *NASCAR* (we have a track in Richmond where I live), you know the difference detail can make in winning or losing. Even something as little as an adjustment of half a pound of tire pressure, or one second longer spent in the pits can mean the difference between winning and losing a race.

In *NASCAR*, details make a huge difference. There are all kinds of little adjustments that can be made on a car, they are just small details but they determine who is winning consistently and who is not. There are millions of dollars being poured into professional racing, and the little details are determining the difference. Teams are hiring engineers who are spending all day, every day, all week long trying to find the little key to make them faster. Attention to detail is so important. Knowing your information and being prepared is crucial to your success. Attention to detail is absolutely critical to being excellent in your career.

Deal Positively with Change

To be excellent at work, you must deal positively with change. Change is a constant in your life, whether you like it or not. People who excel have the right attitude about change. Anyone can get negative under the pressures of unrealistic demands and changing expectations. You can do that, and many people do. Many give in and go negative. They become negative about their job, and that is not a prescription for success and excellence. Christ followers are people who have a can-do attitude. They are not complainers; they do not say, "This isn't fair." They deal positively with the challenges they face.

Those who positively handle change are people who invariably have a better attitude about their work. Bosses change, coworkers change, technology changes. You have to deal with change. There are essentially two ways you can deal with change. One is to be what the psychologists call a benefit seeker. The other is called a consequence avoider. In dealing with change, eighty-five percent of Americans are consequence avoiders rather than benefit seekers. In other words, they change because they have to, because it's forced on them; begrudgingly without a good attitude they change. Maybe the reason you have experienced a career setback is you did not welcome change at your job. A comeback happens when you become a benefit seeker. Benefit seekers are people who look at the benefits that change can bring, who try to identify the positives in any change and choose to focus on the benefits rather than perceived negative consequences. Instead of avoiding perceived negative consequences, they welcome the change with a right kind of mindset and attitude.

I just had lunch with the president of a company this past week and whenever I talk to people who lead the workplace, they almost always talk about change and attitude. They inevitably talk about how much they want a positive attitude out of the people who work for them and how they want them to be change-friendly. Negative attitudes and resistance to change are going to keep you from your comeback. Dealing positively with change is going to drive your career comeback. You must have a positive, change-friendly attitude.

Do More than Is Expected

The final principle of excellence at work is to do more than is expected. This axiom comes from Jesus who said, "If someone asks you to walk one mile, walk another mile." You may have heard the phrase "Go the extra mile" and never knew it was Jesus who taught to go the extra mile. Here is what I know about going the extra mile: there is no traffic jam on the extra mile. Far too few ever travel the extra mile. But this is key for success and excelling in your career: do more than is expected of you. Anyone can do the minimum, anyone can do just what has to be done, but the people who excel are the people who go beyond what is expected. When you do more than is expected you move into new territory, and in that new territory a lot of good things happen. When you get into the extra-mile territory, you get into the creative world. And it is in the world of creativity where so much takes place that ends up blessing your life and our world.

I was at a dinner party recently and I met several new people. I met this person from Milwaukee, Wisconsin, who was visiting some friends and so he came with them to the party. We were talking and I was telling him what I was doing in my life and ministry. He told me how twenty years ago his family had been part of starting a new church and how exciting it had been. We talked about the creative process and how God works when you start something new. We talked about when God's creative energy is at work it's a very exciting place to be. If you've had a setback, if you're kind of bored, why don't you try going the extra mile? Try going into new territory you haven't been before and see if that doesn't spark something inside of you that can create greater excellence.

If you commit to hard work and you commit to excellence, you will have a great career comeback. Putting these principles into practice and practicing them over time, you are going to see a change in your work, your job, your career. You will never have another setback and you will have great success.

HEALTH COMEBACK

One of the great setbacks you can have in life is a health setback. Getting injured, being diagnosed with a disease, or having a lengthy illness can put you in a severe setback position. There are times when nothing you did caused the health problem or nothing you could have done would have prevented the setback. My mother lived a very full and healthy life and then got cancer—twice. My youngest son was a college football star and never got seriously injured playing football but tore his ACL playing basketball. I have had terrible bouts with both kidney stones and gallstones, neither of which I could have done anything to prevent. But there are many health setbacks we can prevent.

The **Centers for Disease Control** tell us over the last fifty years the average American woman has gone from 136 pounds to 166 pounds, the average man has gone from 165 pounds to 195 pounds. There has been an increase of thirty pounds over the last fifty years for both men and women. Extra weight is the cause of many, many health problems. Of all the countries in the world, only Tonga and Micronesia, a couple of islands in the Pacific with some very large people, are heavier than Americans. We are the third heaviest people in the world! The average American is thirty-three pounds heavier than the average Frenchman. The average American is forty pounds heavier than the average Japanese person. Why is this happening? We're eating too much, we're eating the wrong things, and we're not exercising enough.

I Corinthians 6:12–13 says, "Some of you say, 'We can do anything we want to.' But I tell you not everything is good for us. So I refuse to let anything have power over me. You also say, 'Food is meant for our bodies, our bodies are meant for food.' But I tell you that God will destroy them both. We are not supposed to do indecent things with our bodies. We are to use them for the Lord who is in charge of our bodies." Verses 19–20 go on to say, "You surely know that your body is a temple where the Holy Spirit lives. The Spirit is in you and is a gift from God. You are no longer your own. God paid a great price for you. So use your body to honor God."

Your Health Matters to God

The Bible tells us the body is the temple where the Holy Spirit lives. We are no longer our own. God paid a great price for us and we're to use our body to honor God. People who are healthy have less health setbacks. People who can do what they want to do because of good health can make comebacks. People who look in the mirror and like what they see are happier. God created our bodies and they are a good, but when we're not taking care of them the way we should we can have a setback.

Several research studies have shown how people who go to church regularly are healthier people. They have less cardiac problems, they have less disease, and they have less stress. All these physical benefits and more come from going to church, but they discovered one negative about people who go to church: they are heavier than people who don't go to church. Too many Christ followers overeat because that is the one acceptable vice. They don't commit other sins with their body, so gluttony is permitted. They spend more time fellowshipping and less time exercising.

My mother was a dietician and I was an athlete for years so I have some knowledge about healthy living. I have never spent a night in a hospital or had a serious health problem. I have maintained a healthy weight and exercised my entire life. Of course it doesn't mean I'm perfect by any means. My wife recently made chocolate chip cookies for a family in our church that just had a baby. Apparently they needed chocolate chip cookies to help them celebrate. I thought you were supposed to be happy just to have a new baby. I may have sampled a few of those cookies as they made their way out the door.

I love hamburgers but now I only have one a month, but there was a time in my life I would go to McDonald's (which I don't even go to anymore) and eat five hamburgers at a time. In fact one time I ate ten hamburgers, the little ones not a quarter pounder. There are a lot of temptations out there. Richmond, VA, where I live has for whatever reason become the donut capital of the world. Every time you turn around, they're opening a new donut shop. The food temptations are everywhere. Temptation is one thing but sin is another. Being tempted to do something and giving in to it are two different realities.

The ancient church said there were seven deadly sins and two—sloth and gluttony—are directly related to your health. You need to recognize that health is vitally important to your personal happiness and your relationship with God. It's not just about preventing early death. It's about living a better life. How are you going to fulfill your God-given purpose and reach your God-given potential if you leave this earth too soon or you don't have enough energy to do what God has called you to do? A health comeback is the answer.

God Wants Us to Have Healthy Bodies

God wants His followers to be healthy. God cares about your body, not just about your soul. Your health matters to God. One of the errors of the ancient Christian fathers was something called asceticism. This was where they would deny or hurt the body for spiritual purposes. For example, they would put on a mohair vest, not with the mohair on the outside but on the inside with no shirt underneath, and it would rub against their bare flesh where they would feel pain and irritation. It was supposed to help them get closer to God. One spiritual father went up on a pole and stayed there for over 300 days, thinking that was going to make him closer to God. They thought that if they could deny and bring a pain to the body, it would somehow bring them closer to God.

You don't have to punish the body in order to enrich the spirit. God wants us to enrich the spirit while we take care of the body. The Bible tells us the body is the temple of the Holy Spirit. We should take care of the temple God has given us. Someday when you stand before Almighty God to give an accounting of your life, it will not just be the spiritual. It will be how you cared for the one and only body that God gave you. You'll never get another body. We've got to take care of the only one we will ever have.

Fred DeLuca who founded Subway died in 2015 at sixty-seven years old from leukemia. There are more than 44,000 Subway locations around the world. There are more Subways than Starbucks, more Subways than McDonald's. The guy who started it all died far too young. One of the great creative geniuses of all time, Steve Jobs, died prematurely at just fifty-six years old. The founder of Apple and the one who rescued Apple from potential bankruptcy died from cancer in 2011. Michael Hammond, the cofounder of Gateway computers, died in 2015 at fifty-three years old. One of the original personal computer pioneers is gone far too soon. It's an incredible loss to lose people like this who are just fantastic leaders and enriched lives in so many ways. No one is guaranteed health, but we need to do everything we can to take care of the body God has given us.

The **British Medical Journal** says that if you will be physically active, you can add 5.4 years to your life. Physical activity adds over five years to your life. We have become sedentary—and we were not meant to live that way. Exercise and eating right are the keys to a health comeback. **Parade Magazine** reported the chicken sandwich is the new hamburger. Eleven percent of all lunches and seven percent of all dinners ordered in restaurants are now chicken sandwiches. They also listed the five foods we're having more of: yogurt, hummus, fresh fruit, healthy snack bars, and frozen sandwiches. The five foods we're having less of are: soft drinks, cake, steak, corn, and toast. So we are moving in the right direction, but we need to move there faster.

Calorie counting is crucial to a health setback. I have an app on my phone and when I go to a restaurant, I can figure out how many calories of whatever meal I want to order. This is a simple tool to help with eating right. I was in San Francisco a few years ago eating at the Cheesecake Factory. There was a calorie count for every single item on the menu. If you want to ruin a slice of cheesecake, find out it is 1,300 calories. In the same **Parade** article, they showed how calorie counts on menus have a stronger effect on women than men. Forty-two percent of women said that knowing the calorie count would make them order a more healthy meal. Only 29 percent of men said the same thing. Here is another instance of the remarkable differences between men and women. One more hilarious example is the divergence between men and women in changing bedsheets. A single woman changes the sheets on her bed every two and a half weeks. A single guy changes the sheets on his bed once every three months. A guy only changes the sheets four times a year!

Take Responsibility for Your Health

You need to take responsibility for your health. You've got to take personal responsibility. If you're going to be happy, if you're going to have a health comeback, you must take responsibility for your physical well-being. You may think it is too late for you, but the *Cooper Institute in Dallas* did a study showing people who quit smoking by age forty gained nearly ten years of life over those who didn't. Those who started to exercise in middle age were healthier further into old age than those who didn't start exercising. It's never too late. You can start a health comeback right now. The second half of your life can be healthier than the first half of your life. It can happen. You can take responsibility for it.

Healthier living can even improve your memory after fifty. *Duke University* did a study and reported that "physically active older people experience less brain shrinkage than sedentary ones, even those who engage in mentally stimulating activities." In other words, physical exercise is better for your brain than brain exercises. Your health involves many different parts of your life. It's very clear from research that you need seven to eight hours of sleep a night. If you don't get that sleep, it's going to impact your health negatively. God created our bodies to heal themselves and that happens during sleep, not during activity. Sleep matters. The more sleep you get, the happier person you will be, the healthier person you will be. To get more rest, you have to go to bed earlier. I go to bed early, I get up early, and I get a lot done in the early morning hours. It's amazing what adequate sleep can do, but you have to go to bed earlier.

Eliminate Bad Habits

You've got to eliminate bad habits to have a health comeback. Smoking is a bad habit. The Surgeon General has said it will lead to cancer. It's extremely addictive and can have great power over a person. Listen again to what

Paul says: "I refuse to let anything have power over me." Bad habits lead to health setbacks. Drinking is another bad habit. I've never seen anything good come from consuming alcohol. In all my years of ministry, I've personally seen so many problems drinking caused, not to mention the anecdotal and research information on it. These bad habits are no good for you. They don't bring you health and wellbeing.

Mental health is another part of being a healthy person. So many people suffer from depression and they just live with it. God doesn't want you to live with depression. There are multiple therapies that can help lift a person out of depression. You need to take advantage of the right one for you. If you need help, get it—you shouldn't live where you're not mentally well. You can't be a healthy person and be depressed. Depressed people are unhappy. God wants you to be physically and mentally well.

Get Rid of Belly Fat

Visceral fat, which is excess belly fat, nearly doubles a person's risk of premature death because of heart disease, hypertension, stroke, and cancer according to a European study of 360,000 people in nine countries. It nearly doubles your risk of a serious health setback! What is visceral fat? It's the fat around your belly. It's the fat that surrounds all of your vital organs. Visceral fat lies deep inside the abdomen. It surrounds the liver and intestines. Dr. JoAnn Manson, chief of Preventive Medicine at Boston's Brigham and Women's Hospital says, "Visceral fat acts as an active endocrine organ secreting hormones and chemicals that cause chronic inflammation throughout the body. It interferes with cell communication and drains into the liver. It affects liver metabolism and insulin resistance." The fact it surrounds all your major organs and then secretes out the wrong kind of hormones is what makes you sick instead of well. You must get rid of it. It isn't about having a six-pack, flat sexy belly—it's about not having this kind of fat in excess. A man's waist should never be more than forty inches; a woman's waist should never be more than thirty-four inches. Anything larger and there is going to be excess fat harming your body.

Cardio Exercise Is Key

The number one way to get rid of visceral fat is aerobic exercise. A study at *Wake Forest University* found participants who solely dieted lost weight but not belly fat. Cardio exercise burns calories and is the best practice to shrink the visceral fat in your body. The fat has got to go for your health comeback. Of course, it helps your appearance. Does that make you happy? Sure. Most fashionable clothes are made not for heavy people. We have this superheavy country with lots of overweight people and yet the fashionable clothes are for thinner people. The newest fashion for men is "trim fit" in suits and shirts, and there are even "skinny jeans." If you're going to wear these kinds of clothes, you can't have excess fat.

I don't think it is vanity to want to look good. You want to look the way God made you, and God didn't make you to be overweight. God made you to be a healthy weight. When I visited Italy, I climbed up a tower over 400 stairs in Florence and I was behind this overweight woman. The tower was very old and very narrow. She had a terrible struggle as her kids wanted her to go faster. It was not a good situation. She had to stop because she was so winded. When you're healthy, you can be more physically active. Research from **The British Journal of Sports Medicine** suggests regular aerobic exercise may delay or even reverse age-related brain decline, including that associated with Alzheimer's and dementia. A study at the *University of Kansas Medical Center* found high levels of physical fitness have a positive effect on mental plasticity—on the brain's capacity for growth and development. The brain can grow. It doesn't stop. It isn't just about the intellectual stimulation. It's about how physical impacts the mental as well.

Eating Healthy Is Required

Of course you can't get around the eating component for a health comeback. It is crucial. Why do we seem to have such an issue with food? There is more going on than simply the fact that we like food. Some eat for comfort. They are emotional eaters who use food to make them feel better. Some use food as a means of exercising control. They experience disappointments in life and feel too many things are beyond their control, so they eat whatever they want. For some, eating is a distraction from reality. They are bored with life and eat to distract themselves from the mundane nature of their life. And some eat too much believing that big people are jolly people. They eat to present an image of a happy person.

There are many foods you could eat, and there are many you shouldn't eat. We would all like to eat whatever food we want. Eating right is really a matter of planning and discipline. There must be a conscious effort to monitor what we eat. Only as we plan out our meals can we control our eating. Discipline is required to eat smaller portions, to eat healthier foods, and to avoid high-calorie treats. Making those eating changes can be difficult, hard, and challenging, yet they are exactly the step to a health comeback.

I grew up with a little Italian mother who made a lot of pasta, and we had bread and dessert at every single meal—and I mean every single meal. I also grew up playing sports where you burn a lot of calories so you can eat as much as you want. This was before the days of protein shakes and bars. Eating a huge amount of food especially protein was how we built muscle. So I understand what it's like to eat foods that you can't eat for the rest of your life and eating massive quantities of food. Even to this day I could eat a lot of food, but I can't or I will have a health setback.

Set Health Goals

We all have our health challenges. We must make changes and take responsibility. We have to understand the key is to make goals. You need goals for your health just like you need them for other parts of your life. A comeback comes in making progress towards your health goals. Goals are indispensable—they show us what we're capable of overcoming. You may be at middle age, but you can make a change in your life that is going to affect the rest of your life. You're going to be healthier, you're going to live longer, and your brain is going to work better. You're going to avoid another health setback because you decided to make some changes and set some goals.

Goals are not the end—they are means to the end. They help us to get where we need to go. You need to make goals for each area of your health. You refuse to let anything have power over you. You don't do indecent things with your body. You understand your body is the temple of the Holy Spirit. You honor God with your body. Tomorrow is when it starts. Tomorrow is the first day of your health comeback. This is God's desire so you can live as long as possible, be as healthy as possible, and fulfill your God-given destiny.

SPIRITUAL COMEBACK

You may find yourself in need of a spiritual comeback. It could be you have walked away from a personal relationship you once had with Jesus. Maybe a certain sin has taken hold in a life-controlling way and you feel far from God because of it. You may be in a place of spiritual dryness when your prayers seem to hit the ceiling, your desire to go to church has waned, and your interest in spiritual things is almost nonexistent. Good news: you can have a spiritual comeback! In order to do it, we need to look at what the Bible teaches about a spiritual comeback. Terminology is important, so let's begin by defining the term "renewal." You may wonder what the difference is between "renewal" and "revival"?

In many ways they are like the right and the left hand. They are like one side and the other side of a coin. They are different but they are directly related. "Renewal" is when God begins to move first in the life of followers of Christ and in the life of his church. Then that leads to "revival," which is when God begins to move outside of the church and into the culture, the community, the country, the world. This is how I understand those terms, and a spiritual comeback for an individual is renewal.

We have to understand what "renewal" really is. And the Bible has given us a marvelous picture. There are eight renewals in the Old Testament. The New Testament is actually one gigantic renewal. The book of Acts is the story of the move of God in many different places all around the known world. But in the Old Testament you see eight moves of God, eight specific renewals. Of those eight, one gives us the most information. This renewal happened under King Hezekiah. Only David and Solomon in the entire Old Testament have more written about them than Hezekiah. We get the greatest amount of detail about the renewal that comes under the reign of King Hezekiah. We can understand what a "renewal" really looks like by reading II Chronicles 29:1–3, 10, and then II Chronicles 31:20–21.

"Hezekiah was 25 years old when he became king of Judah, and he ruled 29 years from Jerusalem. His mother was Abijah, daughter of Zachariah. Hezekiah obeyed the Lord by doing right, just as his ancestor David had done. In the first month of the first year of Hezekiah's rule, he unlocked the doors to The Lord's temple and had them repaired. So, I have decided to *renew* our agreement with The Lord God of Israel." 31:20–12: "Everything Hezekiah did while he was king of Judah, including what he did for the temple in Israel, was right and good. He was a successful king because he obeyed the Lord God with *all his heart.*"

Last summer our church experienced a spiritual renewal. We decided to have a midweek prayer meeting in June because I was finishing up a series on prayer. The crowd that showed up was three times as large as we had thought would come since school was out. The prayer time was so powerful we decided to have a follow-up Night of Praise two weeks later in July. The turnout for that service in the middle of the summer was amazing, but what happened in that service was far greater. I shared a very brief devotional on the heart. The heart on fire for God is a symbol of renewal. In that service, many people had an encounter with God like they has never had before. A fire was lit in people, and renewal started happening in many ways. We continued to have special services and teaching through the fall. The spiritual comeback some people experienced over the next several months has changed their lives forever.

God revealed himself several times in the Bible through fire. Twice with Moses, including the burning bush, God used fire as a symbol for his presence. The Jesus Culture chorus sums it up well, "Set a fire in my soul that I can't contain, that I can't control, I want more of you God." If we want more of God we will allow God to start a fire in us, then renewal will take place in a powerful way. The symbol or picture of fire has several meanings we need to understand and appropriate in our lives.

Fire Creates Refining

Fire purifies or refines whatever it touches. We need the fire of God to cleanse away anything in our lives that is keeping us from being totally committed to Him. We all have our pet sins and they need to be removed in us. God's fire purifies as it burns away everything that is not pleasing to God. Let the fire of God burn so hot in you that it makes you like gold (Revelation 3:18) that has been put in the fire to remove all impurities so you shine beautifully pleasing to God.

Fire Brings Illumination

Fire brings light into darkness. When the fire of God is burning in us, it will shine so brightly everyone will see it. Jesus taught us, "No one would light a lamp and put it under a clay pot. A lamp is placed on a lampstand, where it can give light to everyone in the house" (Matthew 5:15). When God's fire is burning in us, we will want to share about His love and forgiveness. Evangelistic intensity will be in us and in our church. This renewal will then lead to all-out revival.

Fire Indicates Enthusiasm

We all know what it means to be fired up. When we are enthusiastic, when we have zeal, we have the fire. The fire of God in us means we want more of God, we desire what He wants, we have passion like never before. Zeal for the things of God will amplify a renewal like nothing else can. If you want to see God move in a new and more powerful way, it is because you are on fire for God. Let God fan the flame in you, let it spread to others, and let's see what God can do.

Defining a word is always helpful. "Re" means "again." Anytime "re" is in front of a word, it means "again." So "renew" means *to be new again*. "Rededicated" means to "dedicate again." "Reinstitute" means to "institute something again." So "renewal" is when we are new again. You can see how this word matches so well with a comeback. A comeback is when we come back to where we once were. Renewal is when we are back to the newness of our relationship with God. Our first love—the kind of passion, the kind of excitement, the kind of enthusiasm we once had for God that somehow dissipated is renewed.

What does it mean to be new again? We have in the Bible a picture, a pattern, a process of how renewal takes place. We don't have to wonder about it. We can know exactly what it's like. The key is when Hezekiah said, "I've decided to renew our covenant with the Lord God." It is a decision. You have to decide to be renewed. You have to decide to take the steps to a spiritual comeback. You have to choose to allow God to do something in your life and you commit to it.

Need for Renewal

Why is there a need for a renewal? To understand spiritual renewal, you have to look at what was happening before the renewal began. We have to move back one chapter in II Chronicles to chapter 28:1 to learn about Hezekiah's father, "Ahaz was twenty nine years old when he became the king of Judah, and he ruled from Jerusalem for sixteen years. Ahaz was nothing like his ancestor David." There is a need for renewal when God isn't in first place, when we haven't made God first. David was a man after God's own heart. David put God first. Ahaz did not. There is a need for renewal when other things are more important than God. Only you can decide for yourself if that's true in your life. I'm not as interested in what people say as I am in what people do. So where you go, how you spend your time, and what you spend your money on tells a lot about what's really first priority in your life.

A second reason for renewal is because of disobedience. In verses 2–3 it says, "Ahaz disobeyed the Lord and was as sinful as the kings of Israel. He made idols of the God Baal and he offered sacrifices in Hinnom Valley. Worst of all, Ahaz sacrificed his own sons, which was a disgusting custom of the nations that the Lord had forced out of Israel." Disobedience was far too common. The leader of the people, Ahaz disobeyed the Lord and made idols. Just because we don't have idols fashioned out of stone, gold, or bronze in our homes doesn't mean we don't have idols. We idolize entertainment. It is such a massive idol for so many people, binge-viewing ten episodes of television in a row, going to movies, playing video games, spending hours upon hours, consuming all of this stuff.

In verses 22–24 it says, "Even after all the terrible things happened to Ahaz because he was disobedient, he sinned against the Lord even worse than before. He said to himself, 'The Syrian gods must have helped their kings defeat me. Maybe if I offer sacrifices to those gods they will help me.' That was the sin that finally led to the downfall of Ahaz, as well as the destruction of Judah. Ahaz collected all the furnishings of the temple, smashed them to pieces. Then he locked the doors to the temple."

Ahaz locked the doors to the temple. In other words, he said, "No more church. We're not going to worship anymore." When he locked the doors to the temple, that was when you knew disobedience had reached its limit. Disobedience comes in many shapes and many forms. When sins are not dealt with and you do not repent, there is a need for spiritual renewal. Repentance is not feeling bad. Repentance is not even saying you've sinned. Repentance is when you turn and you go in the opposite direction. The Greek word *metanoia* means to turn and go in the opposite direction you were going. This is what it means to repent.

Another need for renewal comes when the church is in peril. In verse 6 it says, "So the Lord punished them by letting their enemies defeat them. The king of Syria attacked Judah and took many of its people to Damascus." In verse 16 it goes on to say, "Some time later, the Edomites attacked the eastern part of Judah and again carried away prisoners." Our community of faith we call the church is in peril. We are under attack from without and within. People are attending church less. Our younger generation is buying into a whole set of values that are not in keeping with what the Bible teaches. Rationalization has overtaken us so we explain away our wrong behaviors, twist and turn the Bible to say what we want it to mean, rather than simply living by the plain meaning of what the Bible teaches. The church is not expanding its impact. It's not the force and power it should be. Instead of good increasing, evil is increasing. When these things are happening, there is a need for renewal. This is what was happening in Hezekiah's time. There was a need for a comeback then and there is a need for a comeback today.

Steps for Renewal

Hezekiah shows us exactly how a spiritual renewal happens. "Hezekiah obeyed the Lord by doing right, just as his ancestor David had done." Unlike his father Ahaz, who did the opposite of David, Hezekiah said, "I am going to do right like David." And so in the first month of the first year—not the second month, not the twelfth month, and not the second year—Hezekiah unlocked the doors to the Lord's temple and had them repaired. First thing he did—unlocked the doors to the temple.

The first step for renewal is a desire to do right. A desire to be obedient to what the Bible teaches is the first step in a spiritual comeback. Not doing what you want to do, not trying to get around the teachings of the Bible, not trying to rationalize your behavior, but simply having a desire to do right.

This doesn't mean you are doing right, but there is a desire to do right. In the first month of the first year, Hezekiah took one step—he unlocked the doors to the temple. It didn't make everything right, but it was a step in the right direction. If you have a desire to do right, that is the first step for renewal. If you want a spiritual renewal, there has to be a desire to do right. There has to be a desire to obey the teachings of the Bible. The desire has to be there. It is not the only step, but it is the first step to a comeback.

In II Kings 18:4 it tells us, "He (Hezekiah) destroyed the local shrines and tore down the images of foreign gods and cut down the sacred pole for worshipping the goddess Asherah. He also smashed the bronze snake Moses had made. The people had named it Nehushtan and had been offering sacrifices to it."

In order to have a renewal, you have to root out entrenched sin—deeply held sins—your pet sins, your little baby sins, the sins you hold onto. The deep sins are the sins other people don't know about, those that are hidden or those you won't give up doing. The next step to a spiritual comeback is getting rid of persistent sins in your life.

To understand this part of the story, you need to know a little history. In the book of Numbers we are told the Hebrew people were in the desert and poisonous snakes were biting them and they were dying. The people come to Moses and said, "What are you going to do?" And God told Moses to do a very strange thing. He said, "I want you to make a bronze snake and put it on a pole and hold it up and whenever the people look at the bronze snake, they will be healed from their snake bites." This is why in the healthcare field they have the image of two snakes that come together on a pole with the wings on top as their symbol of healing. It comes from this story in the Bible.

The people turned the bronze snake into an idol. I believe the purpose God had for this symbol was it represented a message from God. Just look at the symbol; be reminded of God's power and you will be healed. Focus on God and you'll be healed. The people twisted it all around and made it into an idol. They had kept it and were actually worshiping it. So Hezekiah destroyed it. He also destroyed the other idol to Asherah, a female goddess of fertility. Ancient people wanted to have babies to increase their families and increase the number of their people. This was very important to them and it's even important to this day. Not in the same way it was in ancient times, but people still want to have children.

You may have been following the Lord for five years, you may have been following the Lord for ten years, but you've never dealt with certain sins. And they may not be on the easy-to-see list, they may be deeply entrenched inside of you. There could be issues that are not right but they've never been dealt with until now. Those get dealt with in a renewal, and you get set free from those kinds of bondages. Those issues go out of your life and you are never the same. You are free in a way you have never been before. This happens in a renewal, this is how you have a spiritual comeback.

The third step in a renewal is the restoration of worship. King Hezekiah unlocked the doors to the temple. Then he did something else. In II Chronicles 29 it says, "As soon as Hezekiah gave the signal for the sacrifices to be burned on the altar, the musicians began singing praises to the Lord and playing their instruments. And everyone worshipped the Lord." In a renewal there is a restoration of singing praises to God. Part of how God brings about a renewal is with a restoration of true heartfelt worship. It isn't just going through the motions, we'll clap our hands and maybe we'll raise our hands if we feel like it. There is a real passion to worship God.

The temple was then rededicated. The Passover was reinstated. The Hebrew people had actually stopped celebrating their greatest act of worship remembering God's deliverance through the Passover. Worship is reestablished. They then consecrated the temple. They set themselves apart and said, "We are going to worship God. Worshipping God is more important than anything else. When it's time to worship God, we'll worship God." In a spiritual renewal, you don't have other things you want to do instead of going to church. You go to church, you go to worship Jesus. You schedule your life around worship instead of scheduling your life around other things and then fit worship in.

In a spiritual comeback when you are truly renewed this is what happens. There is an outpouring of generosity. II Chronicles 31: 5–9 tells us, "As soon as the people heard what the king wanted, which was to bring offerings, they brought a tenth of everything they owned, including their best grain, wine, olive oil, honey, other crops. The people from other towns brought a tenth of their herds and flocks as well as a tenth of everything they dedicated to the Lord. The people started bringing their offerings in the third month. And the last one arrived four months later. When Hezekiah and his officials saw these offerings, they thanked the Lord and the people. Hezekiah asked the priest and the Levites about the large amounts of offerings."

Renewal creates generosity in you. You want to give. The high priest Azariah told Hezekiah, "Ever since the people have been bringing us their offerings, we have had more than enough food and supplies. The Lord has certainly blessed His people. Look how much is left over!" You know God has really brought renewal when there is so much money you don't know what to do with all the money God has brought into the church. You give your tithe, you give offerings, you give generously, and worship is powerful. This is what a renewal looks like and the steps that make it happen.

Outcome of Renewal

Having taken the right steps, the outcome of renewal is very exciting. A spiritual comeback always brings joy. II Chronicles 29:30 says, "Then Hezekiah and the officials ordered the Levites to sing the songs of praise that David and Asaph had written. And so they bowed down and *joyfully* sang praises to the Lord." When God moves, when there is renewal, the result is joy. Of course you are joyful. You are right with God and it naturally leads to joy. Marriages are healed, promotions at work happen, and family relationships are restored. All kinds of positive changes happen.

Another marvelous outcome is your faith becomes strong. In II Kings 18:7–8, it says, "The Lord helped Hezekiah so he was successful in everything he did. He even reveled against the king of Assyria refusing to be his servant. Hezekiah defeated the Philistine towns as far away as Gaza—from the smallest towns to the large, walled cities" When you have enormous faith, it is as if God can bring a victory over anything. You look at a problem, an obstacle, and there is such faith it can change. You have this faith because God is moving, you see renewal, and you know God can do it. And God does it.

The final outcome is victory. You have a spiritual comeback! II Chronicles 32:22 tells us, "The Lord rescued Hezekiah and the people of Jerusalem from Sennacherib and also protected them from other enemies. People brought offerings to Jerusalem for the Lord, expensive gifts for Hezekiah, and from that day on, every nation on earth respected Hezekiah." Victory! God keeps moving and working. And when God works, good things happen. There is absolutely no reason why this can't happen today just like it happened in the days of Hezekiah. It happened in our church and it can happen in your life. The only way it can stop is a lack of faithfulness. As long as you're faithful to follow the steps God has clearly spelled out, it will continue. Remember these key words: "And he was successful because he obeyed the Lord God with all his heart."

God will bring a powerful move unlike anything you have ever seen before. There will be so many positive things that take place in your life it will just blow your mind. Your setback will be a distant memory when you experience the victory. This is what it is like to have a spiritual comeback.

COMPLETING YOUR COMEBACK

You now know what to do for a comeback. There is nothing that can stop you. Well, there is actually much that could stop you from completing your comeback, but nothing that can't be overcome through simple persistence. Persevering through the inevitable challenges you face is the way to guarantee your comeback. Don't quit because things are going to change, and they are going to change for the better. I've seen it happen over and over again and I plan on seeing it happen again in the future. If you continue, you will conquer. If you refuse to be discouraged, you will succeed. If you will try one more time, you'll have a great result. You will come back stronger than ever!

If you give up you will miss out. You will never see what God can do. There are so many good things God wants to do in your life, and it's simply a matter of just persevering through. Maybe even today you are just ready to call it quits. You are ready to give up. The dream is over. The setback is just too great and there can be no comeback. Life stinks, life is hard, life is unfair. And then you hear these words of Jesus and you are challenged to think differently. You are challenged to readjust your attitude.

Luke 5: 4–7: When Jesus had finished speaking, he told Simon, "Row the boat out into the deep water and let your nets down to catch some fish. 'Master, Simon answered we've worked hard all night long and have not caught a thing. But if you tell me to, I will let the nets down.' They did it and caught so many fish that their nets began ripping apart. Then they signaled for their partners in the other boat to come and help them. The men came, and together they filled the two boats so full that they both began to sink."

Cast Out Your Nets

Cast out the nets one more time. You are being encouraged through the words and example of Jesus to try again. Peter's response may be like yours, "We've worked all night long! We've worked hard all night long and we haven't caught a thing!" I believe Jesus' words ring true today as they did almost 2,000 years ago. I think that Jesus would say to us: "Cast out your nets again. Do not give up. Do not give in to the disappointment that you may feel. Refuse to have quitting as an option in your life." Peter listened to Jesus and did what he said. And they caught so many fish their nets began ripping apart. They had to signal for their partners to come and help them. Wow! What a comeback, what a turnaround from nothing to more than they could even handle. Fishing was their livelihood; all these fish meant provision for their needs. God will do the same for you.

Every situation is unique. Each person has their own particular circumstances they have to work through. But the persistence principle remains the same for everyone. In the Orient they plant a tree called the Chinese bamboo. For the first four years they water and fertilize the tree with little or no growth. Then in the fifth year after watering and fertilizing, the tree grows to ninety feet in five weeks! The question is: did the Chinese bamboo tree grow to ninety feet in five weeks, or did it grow ninety feet in five years? It grew ninety feet in five years. If at any point during the five years the people had stopped watering and fertilizing the tree, it would have died. Your comeback may be taking longer than you had hoped. You may be tempted to give up and quit trying, but if you will display perseverance, persistence, and endurance, you will have a comeback.

You have to deal constructively with challenges of life. All of us are going to be challenged by disappointments, problems, trials, whatever you may call them. What can you do? Former president Calvin Coolidge said it best, "Nothing in the world can take the place of persistence. Talent will not. Nothing is more common than unsuccessful men with talent. Genius will not. Unrewarded genius is almost a proverb. Education will not. The world is full of educated derelicts. Persistence and determination are omnipotent." You must refuse to give into the challenges of life.

Over a hundred years ago a man named Gale Borden was traveling from America to England by ship. On that journey, two children died because they drank contaminated milk. It upset and bothered him so much he set out to devise a formula where milk could be stored during a long sea passage without getting spoiled. His solution was called condensed milk. You can go to the supermarket and get Borden's condensed milk even to this day. On his gravestone it says this: "I tried and failed. I tried again and again and again and succeeded."

Disarm Your Disappointments

How do you persevere through the challenges? You have to disarm your disappointments. Disarm them. Refuse to allow them to have power in your life or over your life. In the midst of the challenges and disappointments of life, if you can disarm them and not allow them to control your life or impact you negatively, then you can have a comeback. Dwelling on disappointments does nothing to help your comeback. Deny them any place in your conscious mind. Move on, move forward, and move upward towards your comeback.

Life is full of evil. It's full of injustice. It's full of letdowns. Why are there so many challenges? Sin causes problems because you reap what you sow. You do certain things you reap certain realities; other people commit certain sins and they hurt your life. But sinful responses to problems cause more problems. You may have problems because you did something sinful, and your response to what happened is to do another sinful thing that causes you more problems. Don't do it.

Outside influences can cause you challenges. The reality is you can't control what other people do. But outside influences, other people's decisions and choices end up impacting your life. Some of the problems and the disappointments come from what other people do. Some people do some stupid things. Even good people or goodhearted people can do some very foolish stuff. And because you can't control what they do, it ends up impacting you in negative ways.

Choices cause challenges: our own choices, bad judgment, poor decision making. Sometimes we react. Bad reactions can cause a lot of problems. And your good choices can cause you problems. At times choices you make that are good cause you problems, because when you stand up for what's right or you hold people accountable for their actions, they may not react in the best possible way. Then you end up with problems. You did the right thing and you still end up with challenges.

Understand Life Isn't Fair

Life isn't fair. It isn't. But it's reality. Nowhere in the Bible will you ever find the statement that life is fair. You'll never find it. There are unfair things that happen. There are unjust things that happen. And sometimes even when you do the right thing, you end up with the wrong result.

There are times God brings us through certain experiences because he wants us to learn something. Some can be hardheaded and God has to get your attention through a problem or a disappointment. And when he gets your attention you are more open, more willing to listen to His direction for your life. The resistance you may experience on your way to a comeback may have a larger purpose.

In 1987 the Soviet Union was having some problems with their cosmonauts coming back from space suffering dizziness, high pulse rate, and heart issues. The cosmonauts couldn't even walk for days because their muscles had atrophied in the weightless, no-gravity environment. Scientists went to work to solve this problem. They wanted their cosmonauts to be able to spend over two hundred days in space and then function physically when back on earth.

So they designed what they called the "Penguin Suit." It was a suit that had all these elastic bands attached to every part of the suit. Whenever a cosmonaut would make a physical movement, they encountered slight resistance. They sent the cosmonauts into space wearing these Penguin Suits where everything they did in weightlessness required them to push against the resistance of the elastic bands. When they came back to earth after over two hundred days, they found no physical problems whatsoever. No heart problems, no muscle problems, no dizziness—no physical problems at all. The resistance was actually good for them.

Disappointments are life's realities. Discouragement or disarming them is your choice. How you react to them, whether you allow yourself to be discouraged by them or whether you disarm them, is a decision that will greatly impact your comeback. What can you do with the disappointments besides disarming them? You conquer by continuing. You just continue toward your comeback. You refuse to stop. You refuse to give up.

Conquer by Continuing

Maybe you are frustrated your comeback is taking so long or maybe you have lost faith it will ever happen at all. You are thinking about quitting. You are going to quit school. You're not going to go back next semester. College is too hard and too expensive. You are over this friendship. You're sick of it. It's one-sided. You're tired of always giving and never receiving. Tired of being used and misused. Maybe you are done with God. He has not delivered the way He's supposed to. You're not getting what you want in life, you've had just about enough of it. You are through. I would tell you quitting is not the answer. It's never been the answer. It will never be the answer. Quitters never win and winners never quit. You cannot get where God wants you to go if you quit in the middle of the process He is working in your life.

Think where we would be today as a country if Dr. Martin Luther King had quit. He was all of twenty-six years old, a brand-new pastor, when people looked to him to be the spiritual leader of a boycott in Montgomery, Alabama. Why couldn't they get one of the more veteran pastors? This began a one-year boycott. How much persistence and perseverance does it take to go through a yearlong boycott amidst such incredible challenge? At one point he was thrown in jail. A pastor was thrown in jail for standing up for civil rights. He spent eight days in jail for leading justly.

One time he got stabbed at a book-signing. Just signing books for people when someone stabbed him. Think of all the boycotts, sit-ins, and rallies he led. Imagine the amount of stress and pressure he was under trying to bring about social change. How many opportunities did he have to quit? How many opportunities did he have to pass on his leadership role? And yet he persevered. The result was justice for people of color. And he did it all nonviolently. What an example of Christian courage and determination!

You can hang on a lot longer than you think. You don't think you can do it anymore. It's so hard. It's so challenging. But it's darkest before the dawn. Sometimes the toughest it will ever be is right before the breakthrough. It's hard to start over. You may not want to do it. You don't want to risk another disappointment. You've had your heart broken too many times. You can do it. It's going to get better. Who knows what God can do if you persevere? Who knows what God could change? Who knows how a situation that seems so discouraging could turn around?

One of the great achievements of all of human history was the building of the Panama Canal. There was a fairly small piece of land connecting the two giant continents of North and South America. Instead of traveling all the way around South America to get to the other coast of North America, there was the idea of building a canal. The canal would save incredible amounts of time and money. So they began to dig. It's Panama, it's hot, and there are lots of insects. This was hard, hard work. They were digging for a couple of months and all of a sudden there was a collapse and the dirt just poured back into the giant canal they had been digging. Can you imagine how discouraging that must have been?

Thousands of workers digging for over two months with heavy machinery and the whole project fell apart. They turned to Army engineer General George Washington Goethals, who was the leader of the project. He was asked, "What are we going to do?" Goethals did not even hesitate. He didn't even say, "Let me think about it." He just immediately fired back, "Dig it again." He saw no other options; it simply had to be done. And it did get done. It is an unbelievable monument to human invention. It is a time-saving, money-saving canal that changed worldwide commerce. We are the beneficiaries of it all these many years later.

Sometimes you just have to dig it again. You may not want to but you have to. If you don't, then you will never have your comeback. Only by persevering through the problems and challenges can you move past your setbacks.

Become Mentally Tough

Exodus 6: 6-9 says, "Here is my message for Israel. I am the Lord and with my mighty power, I will punish the Egyptians and free you from slavery. I will accept you as my people and I will be your guide. You will know that I was the one who rescued you from the Egyptians. I will bring you into the land that I solemnly promised Abraham, Isaac and Jacob and it will be yours. I am the Lord. When Moses told this to the Israelites, *they were too discouraged and mistreated to believe him.*"

The news was fantastic for the Hebrews. Their slavery was going to be over, accepted as God's people, and delivered into the promise land. But the people's response was unbelief. They could not believe the news. They were too discouraged, too beat up by life to believe and too mistreated to hear things could be better. They lacked mental toughness.

Mental toughness is what allows you to push through hard situations. Mental toughness is what allows you to face adversity. To make the comeback, you've got to have it. There is tension and stress in life. If you can't deal with it, then you are not going to have a comeback. You've got to become a more mentally tough person. Remain optimistic in the face of adversity. Figure out a way to move forward. This is what you do. You keep thinking how you can make it happen. You learn how to respond positively, creatively, and energetically to negative situations.

Anything worth doing is going to involve some degree of pressure, some degree of dissonance. And your comeback is worth attempting. Things aren't always going to be congruent. Everyone's not always going to hop on board. If you're patient, it can work itself out. Just stay mentally tough: if you don't cave, if you don't give into your emotions and do something foolish and just stay strong, it will happen.

Establish Margin

One of the reasons why we are tempted to quit is fatigue. Fatigue attacks our emotions leaving us self-protective, it attacks our bodies leaving us weak, and it attacks our relationships leaving us isolated. Working on a comeback can be exhausting. Reaching a point of overload makes you want to quit.

The answer for overload is *margin.* Dr. Richard Swenson coined the term to describe the amount that is needed in life to be strong. It is the leeway between you and your limits. When you reach the max of your resources or abilities, you have no margin left. Margin is room to breathe, freedom to think, permission to heal. It is time to be able to listen and to love. Margin exists for our relationships—with others and with God. Lack of margin causes us to want to survive instead of thrive. Without margin the temptation to quit is too great.

We live in an overload culture due to our pace of change, our endless activities, our unlimited choices, and information overload. To measure your own margin, increase your demands by ten to twenty percent. If you still thrive you have margin; if you wilt you don't. The four areas of margin are emotional, physical, time, and finances. A lack of margin in any area makes you susceptible to quitting—a lack in more areas means giving up is going to be highly enticing.

Establishing margin or increasing your margin is crucial. Maintaining a balanced life, taking periodic breaks, learning to say no all help. Eating right, exercising regularly, and getting enough rest will aid you in gaining greater margin. Fun activities, monitoring all uses of technology, and consistent church attendance go a long way toward a healthier lifestyle. Your renewed energy will insure you stay persistent and determined to complete your comeback.

As I write this chapter, I am at a beach house graciously provided by a couple in my church on the Outer Banks in North Carolina. Just down the road from here is the Wright Brothers Memorial. There is no greater example of persistence, perseverance, and determination than Wilbur and Orville Wright. They set themselves on a mission to bring manned flight to the world. There could not be two more unlikely heroes than the Wright brothers. As historian David McCullough notes, "They had no college education, no formal technical training, no experience working with anyone other than themselves, no friends in high places, no financial backers, no government subsidies, and little money of their own." Yet, they literally changed the world. Life without air travel is unimaginable and we owe it all to Wilbur and Orville Wright.

They would not allow anything to stop them from their mission. Not failures, not criticism, not even the real risk they could be killed stopped them. They both had crashes that resulted in significant injuries, they struggled financially with little outside help, and they spent years apart in France and America. Their famous first flight was on a winter day in 1903 on a remote, windswept section of North Carolina. Even after their successful flight, many still doubted them and it took years for all their critics to finally acknowledge their greatness. Their unyielding determination was the primary reason they succeeded. Wilbur was a mechanical genius, Orville was fearless, their work ethic was enormous, but their perseverance was decisive.

If you have persistence, determination and endurance, you will complete your comeback. You may lack some money, ability or resources, but a million dollars of determination will get it done. Hebrews 12:1 says, "We must be determined to run the race that is ahead of us." Sometimes we simply persevere by holding on more than not quitting. Winston Churchill once said, "The nose of the bulldog is slanted backwards so he can continue to breathe without letting go."

God never quits. It is impossible for Him to give up on us. Philippians 1:6 says, "He who has begun a good work in you will carry it on to completion." God will always do His part; you just have to do yours. The famous English preacher Charles Spurgeon once said, "By persistence the snail reached the ark." If you keep persisting, you will have your comeback.

MR. COMEBACK 13

Frank Reich is a former football player and presently the offensive coordinator of the Philadelphia Eagles. He was a quarterback who played in both college and the NFL. His unique distinction is that he is known as Mr. Comeback because he led one of the greatest college football comebacks of all time and one of the greatest pro football comebacks of all time. In fact, he is the only person who is named *twice* in ESPN's list of the Twenty Greatest Sports Comebacks.

Frank is an expert on sports comebacks, but he has insights into comebacks of all kinds. I had the opportunity to interview him about comebacks.

Rick: Let's go back to your college career for a moment. You are at the University of Maryland. Tell us about that comeback when you were losing to the University of Miami 31–0. What was that game like, and how did that comeback happen?

Frank: I had spent four years backing up Boomer Esiason, who was a very good quarterback and had a successful pro career. So Boomer graduates, and now I get a chance to be the starter. Well then I got hurt, separated my shoulder, and was out for a number of weeks. We're playing Miami, and we're down thirty-one points, and I had not had a chance to play in the game. I was healthy, but the coach said he didn't want to make another change at QB. I had waited all this time for my chance to play, and then I got hurt. The one thing I really wanted more than anything was taken away from me, and now that I'm ready to come back, the coach won't let me play. We're losing 31–0 at half, and coach comes in the locker room and says, "All right, Frank, you are in the second half."

To be honest, I wasn't thinking, "Hey, we're going to come back and win the game." I was just thinking one play at a time. Let's just go out there and execute the offense, one play at a time. And at the end of the day, that's one of the really big lessons I've learned about comebacks. When the circumstances, when the scoreboard, whether it's life or football, seem overwhelmingly against you, the lesson I've learned repeatedly is one play at a time, one day at a time.

Rick: So to go from a setback to a comeback does not happen overnight; it's a process. And whether it is football, finances, your marriage, your job, or your health, it is going to be a step-by-step, day-by-day process.

Frank: I agree one hundred percent. I was very blessed to have grown up in a great family. I can remember one story. I'm a little boy, and my dad sends me out in the backyard with a wheelbarrow and a shovel. And he tells me that before I could go out and play with my friends, I have to move this pile of dirt basically across the yard. It was like two dump truck loads. I mean it was huge, and I was just nine or ten years old. I told my dad I could not do it. I went back and forth throughout the day to my dad, and every time I would complain he would say, "Frank, one shovel full at a time, one wheelbarrow full at a time." The lesson I learned that day, which I think was part of the foundation for this game, was there was a mountain of dirt to be moved one shovel at a time. Many times I think we look for that instantaneous moment where life can just be completely turned around. And sometimes that does happen. But a lot of times—for me most of the time—it's been one shovel full at a time, one decision at a time.

Rick: I think all of us want the miracle. We want the instant healing from the physical problem or the instant financial blessing so that we're out of the woods. But it mostly happens in a different way. God can do anything, but He usually takes you step-by-step. Let's go back to the Maryland game. So you get in the game with Miami. What happens?

Frank: I start the second half, and I don't remember exactly, but its three or four plays, and we hit a touchdown pass. Now another thing I have learned about a comeback, and this is one of the great things about football, is it's not just one guy. Okay, we scored a touchdown, but if our defense doesn't now go out there and stop them, it's all for naught. And so our defense goes and stops them, and then the next thing we score another quick touchdown. And all of a sudden, where it seemed like we had no chance, now maybe we do. You could feel the momentum, but again it was just one play at a time. We were executing a run here, making a pass there, and the defense was playing well. You could feel the people in the stands saying, "What's going on here?"

Rick: Let's talk about momentum. I think every comeback has to have momentum. And it's amazing how momentum can almost make you better than you are. When you have it, it's the greatest thing you could have in your life. What is it like when you have the momentum and the other team does not?

Frank: Well, it's huge. I think for me my experience has been that momentum has a foundation, and the foundation is your preparation, your previous battles, and your previous journey. It is my childhood while growing up. It's the teammates, it's the practice, it's all that stuff going in that prepares you for the moment in time when momentum is there. Can you capitalize on it? Can you take that step? Can you throw that pass? Can you make the right decision?

Rick: Tell us about your preparation. Tell us a little bit about how you grew up in Pennsylvania.

Frank: My mom and dad were high school teachers. My dad was a football coach. But my dad was one of those coaches who never forced me to play. He didn't even tell me when football tryouts were. I had to find out from my buddies. One time when I was snooping around like a ten- or eleven-year-old boy will do, I found these big paper bags in my parent's closet, and I pulled them out. I had never seen them before, and there were two big scrapbooks. I discovered that my dad was the captain of the Penn State football team. He was an All–American, and I never even knew this!

Rick: Wow.

Frank: So my dad comes home and I said, "Dad, what's the deal here?" He said, "I never wanted you to feel like you had to play football if you didn't want to." He was just a great role model for me, a great example. He loved me unconditionally. So when I started playing, I never really felt the pressure from my dad. I felt like he was going to love me and support me whether I was a good football player or a terrible football player. His one rule was you give one hundred percent to whatever you do, and if you start a season, you finish a season.

Rick: So part of a comeback is keeping focused on where you want to get to and not giving up for any reason. Not allowing the many distractions in life to keep you from your goal.

Frank: Absolutely.

Rick: So how do you end up going to Maryland instead of Penn State if your dad was at Penn State?

Frank: Excellent question. Penn State recruited me, but Penn State also had a reputation for taking high school quarterbacks and making them into linebackers. I knew that I couldn't play any other position other than quarterback, so I went to Maryland. I just kind of felt like Maryland was the right place for me.

Rick: When you get there, one of the best quarterbacks to play the game, Boomer Esiason, ends up being on your team, and so you have to wait your turn.

Frank: Yeah, we ended up being the best man in each other's weddings. So here I am competing against this guy, sitting on the bench behind him, but yet we're real close friends.

Rick: And then you both ended up playing in the NFL.

Frank: Yes.

Rick: So finish out the Miami game for me. The defense is doing its job. The O line's doing its job. Did Miami ever even score again?

Frank: They scored one time late. In fact, it was 31–0 at half. Then we got to the point where we were up 42–31, and they kick a field goal somewhere in the second half, so it was now 42–34. They actually got the ball back and scored to make it 42–40 with just a couple minutes to go. They go for the two-point conversion and have a chance to tie the game, and we stop them.

Rick: And that is how you won the game. You scored forty-two points in one half of football.

Frank: Yes. That was the comeback.

Rick: Wow. So then how did you get in the NFL?

Frank: I only ended up starting six games in my entire college career. And yet I was drafted by the Buffalo Bills in the third round. I was sitting in my college room with my girlfriend, who's now my wife, waiting for that phone call on draft day. I knew I wasn't going to be a high draft pick, but they told me I'd probably be drafted somewhere in the second or third round, and I was the first player taken in the third round. We weren't engaged, but we had been dating for like four years. I think we both knew at that point that we would get married and this was going to be our life. We had decided that it was going to be great to play in the NFL anywhere. Her words were, "I just pray it's anywhere but the Buffalo Bills." So I get that phone call. I pick up the phone, and the man said, "This is Kay Stephenson, the head coach of the Buffalo Bills." I was thinking, "You got to be kidding me!" And she was in the background going, "Who is it? Who is it?" And I go, "It's Buffalo!" She started crying.

Rick: Okay. So you get to Buffalo.

Frank: There were two or three guys on that team that I ended up becoming close with who had a big impact on my life. So I thank God he took us to Buffalo.

Rick: Tell me about the Oilers game, because the game is legendary. It is one thing to have a comeback in the regular season, and it is another thing in the playoffs. Just take us into the pregame, the team mentality, and then as the game progresses.

Frank: Well, what most people don't know is in the last week of the regular NFL season, we played the Houston Oilers at Houston. If we won that game, we were going to get a bye. The short story is Jim Kelly got hurt in that game. I came in, played really badly, and we lost 28–3. As a result of losing, we now don't get a bye, and we play the Oilers again the next week. Because they beat up on us the first time, now everything in the media is that the Oilers have the momentum.

Rick: Jim Kelly, the All-Pro QB, is hurt, and you played a terrible game the previous week.

Frank: Yes, Kelly is hurt, I played poorly, and people were not giving us a chance. Then we come out in the first half, and Warren Moon is lighting it up, and they are winning 28–3 at halftime. Now do the math. If they beat us 28–3 the week before, and now they are beating us 28–3 again, cumulatively it is 56–6.

Rick: That is bad.

Frank: Oh, it gets worse. We get the ball to start the second half, and I throw an interception that is returned for a touchdown on my first pass. So that now makes it 35–3.

Rick: Did you say, "Guys, don't worry. I've done this before"?

Frank: No.

Rick: You did not say that?

Frank: No, I did not say that. Because the Maryland-Miami game was a big game, and there were guys on the sidelines who knew. I do think that was a factor for me at least in the game.

Rick: You had confidence.

Frank: The confidence to know if we're going to come back from thirty-two points, it doesn't all happen at once. It's going to take everybody on this team, and we've just got to execute one play at a time.

Rick: By your own admission, you did not play well in that final regular season game. You didn't really play that well in the first half.

Frank: Yeah, that's right.

Rick: How do you have confidence for the comeback with those kinds of setbacks? How do you restore your confidence?

Frank: It is a matter of preparation. There is a great quote that I remember from a famous general. He is talking to his men before they go into battle, and he says, "You know, you can determine the manner of man you will be whenever and wherever you get called into action. Because no man becomes suddenly different from his habit and cherished thought." I do believe that extraordinary things happen when ordinary people maintain a consistency, have a belief, and have some conviction.

Rick: So confidence is important.

Frank: It is really important. But I've learned through football that some of the times I find confidence in my greatest humiliations and being down that low, and then realizing I'm not in control. That it takes teammates; it takes a whole team for something like this to happen. It takes support.

Rick: So how did you do it? How did you have such an incredible comeback?

Frank: So it was 35–3. We go down, and we have a pretty quick score, and now it's 35–10. We then have the surprise onside kick. That was really one of those great calls by our head coach. To be thinking that far in advance that if there is going to be a comeback, we're going to have to take a chance and do something out of the ordinary. It was a great call by our head coach, Marv Levy, and we executed it perfectly. That call really kind of ignited something in our team. Three plays later, I throw a touchdown pass to Don Beebe. Warren Moon throws an interception. A few plays later, I throw another touchdown pass. Now it is 35–24. Only like six minutes had gone by in the game, and everybody is like, "Wow!"

Rick: Now it is a game, and there is plenty of time left.

Frank: There is plenty of time left. And we just kind of kept rolling. Between each series, I'm over on the sidelines, pacing back and forth, humming the words to the song "In Christ Alone" that my sister had called me that week and told me about. If you want to have a comeback, you can come partway back and then all of a sudden get caught up in the excitement and the momentum. You have got to stay doing what you've been doing that got you there. And we did get there because we ended up going into overtime, where we won on a field goal. So we came back from the biggest deficit in NFL playoff history.

Rick: Right.

Frank: So part of the way I stayed focused was just kind of humming that song, because the words gave me a quiet confidence. Not that God was going to be on my side and everything was going to work out how I wanted it, but it just gave me a quiet confidence. And that is why after the game was over at the press conference I quoted that song.

Rick: Because it was that significant.

Frank: Yes.

Rick: Tell me about your faith and your spiritual journey. Where did it all start?

Frank: Well, as God has it sometimes, he takes ordinary people in ordinary circumstances. I was involved in football a lot. I grew up in football, so football was primary in my life. I waited, backed up Boomer Esiason for four years, and then when I finally get my chance I get hurt, and now everything is taken away from me. My dream of playing in the NFL is gone. I recover from my injury, but now the guy who took my place had been playing well, and the coach isn't going to let me play. I'm done. It's over.

Rick: At twenty-two years old.

Frank: Yeah. I mean, for me, it's over. I can laugh at that now, but when you are twenty-two and this is your life, it is real. Football was everything to me, and I thought it was taken away. There was a minister on campus with Campus Crusade for Christ who had been kind of telling me some things. My girlfriend, who is now my wife, was telling me things in my other ear, "You know, Frank, you need to kind of just think through this and get your priorities straight and think about your relationship with the Lord." So it was in those moments in college, going through that difficult time, that I said, "Okay, God. You got my attention. I'm giving my life to you. I'm surrendering my life to you. Forgive me of my sin. And, Jesus, I do believe you are who you say you are, and I'm going to commit my life to following you."

Rick: So then where does it go from there?

Frank: I'm kind of wallowing around. I'm at chapel on Sundays, and then I'm out in the bars doing my own thing early on in my Christian days. My life really hadn't changed a whole lot, but a little bit. God was very gracious to put some really strong men in my life, including a team chaplain. He invited me to start coming to Bible study and getting involved.

Rick: So you have a nice long career in the NFL.

Frank: Yes, fourteen years. One other really quick note about the comeback game that I think is important. After our comeback game, we are playing in Super Bowl XXVII against the Cowboys. Jim Kelly had started that game. When I came into the game, we were losing 17–7, and I'm thinking, "We're going to come back and win this game." A month before we were down by thirty-two, now we're only down by ten. I quoted that song after that game. Now God's going to bless me with a Super Bowl victory, and I might even be the MVP!

Rick: Wow! Okay.

Frank: Well, the long story short is that we lost 52–17. I am a Super Bowl record holder—I hold the record for the most fumbles in a Super Bowl game. And I threw a couple interceptions too, by the way. So it wasn't just the fumbles. So in a course of one month, I go from the highest of highest to the lowest of the lowest. But the lesson through that is being consistent.

Rick: There are lessons to be learned from setbacks and from comebacks. Your stories are fantastic; they are an encouragement and an inspiration. Thank you, Frank.

TOP TEN GREATEST COMEBACKS OF ALL TIME

In choosing ten comebacks as the greatest of all time, some standard was necessary for arriving at such an auspicious list. My criteria involved two elements, and within each element a measurement was used. The elements were the nature of the setback and the prominence of the comeback. The measurement for each was simply the greatness of the span between the setback and the comeback.

There have been many great comebacks in history. This book is devoted to the concept that there can be many more. But there are certain comebacks that simply stand apart from all others because of their greatness. My top ten list begins with number ten.

Robert Downey Jr.

Robert Downey Jr. had a great amount of success at a young age. He starred in a number of films throughout the

1980s and 1990s, receiving an Academy Award nomination for best actor in the 1992 film, *Chaplin*.

After this promising start, Robert began to face problems in his personal life. From 1996–2001, he was arrested numerous times on drug-related charges. In April 1996, he was arrested for possession of cocaine, marijuana, and an unloaded .357 Magnum while speeding down Sunset Boulevard. He was sentenced to three years' probation and required to undergo mandatory drug testing.

But that first arrest did not stop his destructive behavior. A year later, he missed a court-ordered drug test and had to spend four months in the Los Angeles County jail. Even jail time failed to change Robert's behavior and in 1999, he missed another drug test and was sentenced to three years at the California Substance Abuse Treatment Facility and State Prison in Corcoran, California. He received a big break when he was unexpectedly released early for previous time served in 1996.

Unfortunately, Robert's addiction was too strong, and he was arrested yet again the following year for possession of cocaine and Valium. In July 2001, he pleaded no contest to the charges but avoided jail time because of California's Proposition 36, which was aimed at helping nonviolent drug offenders to overcome addiction through court-ordered rehabilitation.

Downey told Oprah in 2004 that he finally decided he needed help and reached out for it. He said, "You can reach out for help in a kind of half-assed way and you'll get it, and you won't take advantage of it. It's not that difficult to overcome these seemingly ghastly problems ... what's hard is to decide to actually do it." After five years of setbacks, he decided he was going to have a comeback.

While he managed to stay employed with small projects throughout his battle with drug addiction, it was in 2008 when his career comeback solidified. He was nominated for Best Supporting Actor for his role in *Tropic Thunder*. He landed the lead role in the movie *Iron Man*, and *Entertainment Weekly* named him "Entertainer of the Year."

In addition, *Time* named him one of the 100 Most Influential People of 2008.

Robert now has the lead role in two widely successful movie franchises, *Iron Man* and *Sherlock Holmes*. In 2010, his role as Sherlock Holmes earned him a Golden Globe for Best Performance by an Actor in a Motion Picture. Downey is one of the most popular and sought-after actors in Hollywood, solidifying his comeback. He has also started a foundation to help others.

Josh Hamilton

Josh Hamilton was the first overall pick in the 1999 Major League Baseball draft by the Tampa Bay Devil Rays, receiving a $3.96 million dollar signing bonus. He was an unlikely candidate as a future drug addict but, unfortunately, adversity struck his life and young career in the form of numerous injuries.

In 2001, Josh was involved in a car accident that placed him on injured reserve. In his first three seasons, he missed a total of 236 games because of injuries. During this time, he self-medicated with drugs and alcohol. As a result, he tested positive for substance abuse, was suspended, and put into a treatment program.

However, this did not stop his addictive behavior. In 2004, Major League Baseball suspended him indefinitely for violating the joint drug treatment and prevention program. At this point, he had become a full-blown addict; the substance abuse as a coping mechanism for his injuries and that stalled his promising career had become the agent of his career destruction. His depression worsened.

Finally, in 2005, he hit rock bottom, waking up on his grandmother's doorstep after what would be his final crack cocaine binge. Hamilton had experienced a gigantic setback, and his future was very dim.

He chose a road that led to recovery and his comeback in baseball. In an ESPN article about his story, Josh describes his comeback: "It's a God thing. It's the only possible explanation." In that same article, he describes two dreams that encompassed his journey back from addiction:

I was fighting the Devil, an awful-looking thing. I had a stick or a bat or something and every time I hit the Devil, he'd fall and get back up. Over and over I hit him, until I was exhausted, and he was still standing.

I woke up in a sweat, as if I'd been truly fighting, and the terror that gripped me makes that dream feel real to this day. I'd been alone for so long, alone with the fears and emotions I worked so hard to kill. I'm not embarrassed to admit that after I woke up that night, I walked down the hall to my grandmother's room and crawled under the covers with her. The Devil stayed out of my dreams for seven months after that. I stayed clean and worked hard and tried to put my marriage and my life back together. I got word in June 2006 that I'd been reinstated by Major League Baseball, and a few weeks afterward, the Devil reappeared.

It was the same dream, with an important difference. I would hit him, and he would bounce back up, the ugliest and most hideous creature you could imagine. This devil seemed unbeatable; I couldn't knock him out. But just when I felt like giving up, I felt a presence by my side. I turned my head and saw Jesus, battling alongside me. We kept fighting, and I was filled with strength. The Devil didn't stand a chance.

You can doubt me, but I swear to you I dreamed it. When I woke up, I felt at peace. I wasn't scared. To me, the lesson was obvious: Alone, I couldn't win this battle. With Jesus, I couldn't lose.

Josh's reinstatement was just the beginning of his remarkable comeback. In 2008, he was selected to his first All-Star team, where he also participated in the Home Run

Derby, setting an opening round record of twenty-eight home runs and finishing with the second most home runs of all time in Derby history with thirty-five. His Home Run Derby explosion introduced Josh to the public in a big way, furthering his comeback.

Josh has been selected to the All-Star team for three straight years (2009–2011.) In 2010, he won several single-season honors in the American League, including the batting title, ALCS MVP, and most impressively, MVP of the entire American League.

The man who almost lost his life and career to addiction became one of baseball's biggest stars. In addition to his personal success, he has led his team, the Texas Rangers, who had never won an American League pennant, to two American League pennants (2010–2011) and World Series appearances.

Josh's comeback is still continuing. Only in time will his full success be known.

Ulysses S. Grant

Grant was both a general and a president. He was an American hero in the truest sense of the word. Misunderstood by many people who don't know his whole story, his life is a powerful example of a comeback.

Grant was the son of a tanner in Ohio. He was soft-spoken and easily embarrassed. He went to West Point and entered into the Army as an officer. He served in the Mexican-American War and then was sent to the new Oregon territory out west. He did not like it; he did not like the climate, and he did not like being separated from his wife and children. In his depression, he drank too much, quit the Army, gave up his officer commission, and went back home.

Grant tried his hand at a couple of different things and failed at both real estate and business. He was working in his family's tannery, making very little money, when the Civil War broke out. The Union Army contacted him, since he was a West Point graduate and had combat experience in the Mexican-American War, and asked to rejoin the Army, which he did.

He actually did not do well in his first battle, but then he had a great victory at Fort Donaldson, and then he won a big battle at Shiloh, which got the attention of President Lincoln. Lincoln kept going through generals, trying to find somebody who actually would get the job done, and he decided that Grant was someone who would actually fight.

Grant kept getting promoted until he was the top general of all the Union forces. He won the Civil War not by fancy maneuvers or clever strategy, but by confronting the Confederate Army in the field and defeating it. The man with the rumpled uniform, unkempt beard, and ever-present cigar accepted the surrender from General Lee of the Confederate forces at Appomattox.

Grant was then elected as president of the United States. In fact, he was reelected twice, serving two terms as president. Though his two terms were riddled with political and financial scandals (none directly involving him), he managed to bring a calming influence to the country and bring peace between the North and South and between the US and the rest of the world.

The culmination of Grant's comeback was his memoirs that he wrote after he left the presidency. He wrote *Memoirs*, a book about his life which, at the time, became the best-selling book in American history, excluding the Bible. The shy boy from humble beginnings who failed at much in the early part of his life had an incredible comeback. He was the top general that led the Union's victory in the Civil War, was elected president for two terms of the United States, and wrote the best-selling book of all time.

Kurt Warner

Kurt Warner is a Super Bowl champion, two-time National Football League MVP, and Hall of Fame candidate. His journey to success consisted of many setbacks and two remarkable comebacks. Throughout his incredible journey, he has always given credit to his faith in Jesus Christ as the foundation for his success.

After his college football career at the University of Northern Iowa, Warner went undrafted in the 1994 NFL draft. He was invited to try out for the Green Bay Packers but was released before the start of the regular season. With no other options, he took a job working at a grocery store in Cedar Rapids, Iowa, making $5.50 an hour. He also worked as a graduate assistant coach for the Northern Iowa football program while waiting for another NFL opportunity.

No NFL team was willing to give him an opportunity, so he signed with the Arena Football League's Iowa Barnstormers in 1995. During his two seasons in the AFL (1996 and 1997), Warner was named first team All-Arena and led his team to two Arena Bowl appearances. Finally, the Saint Louis Rams signed him in 1998, but they allocated him to the NFL Europe's Amsterdam Admirals, where he led the league in touchdowns and passing yards. After that season, he came back to the Rams as their third-string quarterback.

The 1999 season would change the course of Warner's life and career. The Rams' starting quarterback, Trent Green, tore his ACL in a preseason game, and Warner became the starter. Up to this point in his career, he had never been a starter in the NFL and had actually played very little. That year, he would have one of the all-time best single seasons by a quarterback, throwing for 4,353 yards with forty-one touchdown passes and a completion rate of 65.1 percent.

Warner led the Rams' high-powered offense known as the "greatest show on turf" to a Super Bowl victory over the Tennessee Titans. In that game, he threw for a Super Bowl record 414 yards and was named the Super Bowl MVP. In addition, he would become the seventh player to win both the league MVP and Super Bowl MVP in the same season.

Warner won a second league MVP in the 2001 season when he again led his team to the Super Bowl, where they lost to the Patriots. In a close game decided by three points, Warner threw for the third highest passing total in Super Bowl history.

After winning two MVPs in three seasons, Warner suffered another setback when he injured his throwing hand and did not complete the 2002 season. In 2003, he was replaced as the starter after fumbling six times in the season-opening game. He was released the next season and signed a two-year contract with the New York Giants. His setback continued as he was replaced in the middle of the season by the highly touted rookie, Eli Manning. At the end of the season, Warner decided to void the second year of his contract and become a free agent.

In 2005, Warner signed a one-year contract with the Arizona Cardinals. He started most of that season and had a good enough year that he signed a three-year extension the following year. The Cardinals then drafted quarterback Matt Leinart out of the University of Southern California, who replaced Warner in week four of the 2006 season. For the second time in his career, Warner was replaced by a rookie quarterback even though he was a two-time MVP and Super Bowl winner.

Leinart was named the starter again in 2007 but was ineffective, and Warner regained the job later in the season. Despite Warner's success, there was a quarterback controversy in the off-season. Eventually, Warner was named the starter, where he led the Cardinals to a division title, their first playoff appearance since 1998, and then the Super Bowl against the Pittsburgh Steelers. The Cardinals lost a very close game, but Warner threw for 377 yards, making him the record holder for the top three passing yard totals in Super Bowl history.

Warner retired as a four-time All-Pro, having played in three Super Bowls and thrown over one hundred touchdowns for two different teams. His outstanding play in the playoffs make him one of the best clutch players in NFL history, and his off-field accomplishments culminated in his being named the 2008 NFL Man of the Year. Twice tossed aside as not good enough to start in the NFL, Warner's comebacks are truly remarkable.

Serena Williams

Serena Williams' tennis career has been nothing short of phenomenal. She rose up from meager beginnings in Compton, CA, to become the world's number one female tennis player in 2002. Serena won twenty-two Grand Slam singles titles and teamed with her sister Venus to win fourteen Grand Slam doubles titles as well. In 2003 she won four consecutive Grand Slam tournaments and established herself as a great champion. She continued her incredible career having just won her fourth Wimbledon tournament in July 2010 when she stepped on broken glass while leaving a restaurant in Germany and injured a tendon in her right foot.

She had surgery to repair it and planned to return to tennis in the fall. But she reinjured her foot and had a second operation in October of that year. Then in February 2011, she suffered a pulmonary embolism (a blood clot in her lung) after flying from New York to Los Angeles. She saw her doctor, who performed a CT scan of her lungs and discovered the blood clot. Serena had been immobilized for six months in two different casts after her foot surgeries. Being sedentary allowed blood to pool in the legs, increasing the risk of a clot that can move to other parts of the body.

A few weeks later, Serena developed a hematoma (a pocket of blood that swells under the skin) in her stomach. It happened after she gave herself an injection of blood-thinning medication that had been prescribed to treat the clots in her lung. She hit a blood vessel and her blood didn't clot so she started bleeding on the inside. The hematoma started out being the size of a golf ball but ended up being the size of a grapefruit. Serena was rushed to the hospital where doctors had to remove the hematoma surgically.

The multiple health scares took a toll on the tennis star. She couldn't function like normal—playing tennis, driving, working out, even walking. Serena spent a lot of time at home during her recovery. It wasn't easy for a person who was used to going 200 mph every day. She was very discouraged and there was a time she didn't even leave the house for two days at her lowest of lows. Serena's health struggles brought her to a place where she considered whether she might never play tennis again or play it at the highest level.

Her comeback began in mid 2011. Over the next four years Serena would win 8 grand slams. She won the gold medal in 2012 Olympics. She was the WTA Tour champion in 2012, 2013, 2014, and 2015. She became the oldest player to reach and hold world number one and to win a Grand Slam tournament. In a sport known for extreme youthfulness, Serena dominated women's tennis while in her thirties. In 2015 she again completed the "Serena Slam," winning all four Grand Slam tournaments consecutively. Her comeback success has been as great as her success before her setback, and considering her age is actually even greater.

To complete her amazing comeback, she was named the Sports Illustrated Sportsperson of the Year 2015, becoming the first solo woman to receive the award since 1983. Serena won the 2017 Australian Open for her 23rd major setting the record for the most majors by a woman.

Postwar Germany and Japan

The aftermath of World War II left Germany and Japan devastated. Most of their large cities were severely damaged, along with the countless lives lost. There were shortages of food and lack of housing and transportation. In addition to all of this was the humiliation of defeat. The worldwide view of these nations was one of disdain as evil empires whose aggression had caused another world war.

Both Germany and Japan had truly experienced a national setback. Both governments and economies were completely restructured by postwar occupation by the Allied Forces. The ramifications of this left both countries in far worse shape than their prewar conditions. Their comebacks are known as the postwar economic miracle. Germany and Japan are now the third and fourth largest economies in the world, respectively.

By the end of the war, Japan had lost two million lives, and over one hundred cities were destroyed. Industrial production stood at less than ten percent of its prewar level. The United States occupied Japan from 1945–1952, during which time it brought demilitarization, democratization, as well as industrial, land, and education reform.

The Korean War propelled Japan's economy into recovery, as it became the principal supplier of food and arms for the US armed forces. During this period industry was rejuvenated and, by 1955, industrial output was back to its prewar level.

Japan began rebranding itself by abandoning militarism and focusing on becoming an industrial and technological nation. Much of modern technology (HD televisions, DVD players, audio equipment) has been invented or made in Japan. According to the Japanese economist Ryuotaro Komiya, Japan's overriding goals have been making the economy self-sufficient and catching up with the West. Japan's postal savings institution has fostered a high savings rate, reducing the cost of capital and allowing debt to be financed internally. They have also developed a highly efficient workforce through their rigorous education system. Ultimately, from 1950–1980, Japan's economy grew at a remarkable rate of ten percent annually.

By 1948, the German people had been living under price controls for twelve years and rationing for nine. Hitler had imposed price controls for his own economic gain, resulting in severe food shortages and high inflation. The end of the war meant the end of these policies, thus unleashing industrial productivity.

In just the first six months, industrial production had increased by fifty percent. The split of Germany into the Communist East and the Democratic West in 1961 concentrated economic growth solely in the West, where it stalled from decreases in the labor force that accompanied the split.

The reunification of Germany in 1990 brought about another comeback, as there were now plentiful laborers for their various industries. At the core of Germany's successful comeback was its highly efficient industrial sector. Germany's economy now excels above all other European countries.

Buffalo Bills: 1993 Playoff Game

The Buffalo Bills played the Houston Oilers in an NFL playoff game in 1993, where the Bills recovered from a thirty-two-point deficit to win the game in overtime. The Bills' comeback was the greatest postseason comeback in NFL history.

The Oilers had beaten the Bills 28–3 the week before, which cost them a first-round bye in the playoffs. In the first half of the game, the Oilers continued their domination over the Bills. Quarterback Warren Moon went 19–22 for 220 passing yards and four touchdowns to put the Oilers up 28–3 at halftime. Just 1:41 into the second half, Bills quarterback Frank Reich threw an interception that was returned for a touchdown, putting the Oilers up 35–3. On top of their thirty-two-point deficit, the Bills lost their star running back, Thurman Thomas, to a hip injury.

The Oilers kicked off with a squib kick that was very poor, giving the Bills excellent field position. The Bills drove the short field and scored their first touchdown. In what may have been the turning point of the game, the Bills then tried an onside kick and were successful in recovering the ball. Just four plays later, Reich hit Don Beebe with a thirty-eight-yard touchdown pass. The Bills then forced the Oilers to punt for the first time in the game, resulting in just a twenty-five-yard punt. The Bills scored again on a touchdown pass from Reich to Andre Reed, and all of the sudden the score was 35–24.

Ten minutes into the third quarter, the Bills had scored twenty-one points and the Oilers had only run three plays for three yards. The Bills then intercepted Moon and scored on a fourth down attempt with another touchdown pass to Reed. In the fourth quarter, the Bills scored another touchdown on a pass to Reed, and now the Bills were actually ahead of the Oilers 38–35. Moon led the Oilers on a sixty-three-yard drive, resulting in a field goal that tied the score and sent the game into overtime.

The Oilers won the coin toss and could have won the game without the Bills ever even getting the ball, but Moon threw an interception. Reich led the Bills down the field, where they kicked a thirty-two-yard field goal to win the game. In just one half of a game and a little overtime, the Bills erased a thirty-two-point setback and produced the greatest comeback professional football has ever seen. And they did it in the playoffs.

Boston Red Sox 2004 Playoff

The Boston Red Sox is one of the most famous professional sports franchises in America. Its popularity has created the Red Sox Nation, where people from all over the world, not just New England, follow them fanatically. Their fan base has grown even larger since they pulled off the greatest baseball playoff comeback in history.

The Sox had a successful beginning to their franchise, including winning the very first World Series. They went on to win four more world championships by 1918, and the future looked very bright for years to come. However, after 1918, they did not win another World Series for eighty-six years. It was called the "Curse of the Bambino" since, after they traded Babe Ruth to the hated New York Yankees, they never won another world championship. They played in four World Series but never won, even with some of the greatest baseball players ever like Ted Williams and Carl Yazstremski.

In 2004, the Sox played their rival, the New York Yankees, in the American League Championship series. They had lost to them in the same series the previous year. The Red Sox began the series by losing the first two games, and then in game three, they lost 19–8 at home, which was the worst playoff loss in Red Sox history. They were now down 3–0, and no team in Major League Baseball history had ever come back from a 3–0 deficit to win a postseason series.

Game four went into extra innings and was won by the Red Sox on a walk-off homer by David "Big Papi" Ortiz. Game five also went into extra innings and was won when Ortiz hit an RBI single. The Red now had to go back to unfriendly Yankee stadium for game six after having barely escaped in the last two games, knowing they still would lose the series if they lost one more game.

The Red Sox won game six thanks in large part to the pitching of Kurt Schilling, despite having stitches in his ankle. In game seven, for the first time, the Yankees were in danger of losing the series. Incredibly, they did lose the game *and* the series. The Boston Red Sox had overcome the greatest deficit in baseball history against their most-hated rival to have a comeback like no other in playoff baseball.

However, the comeback was not yet complete. The Sox still had to win the World Series in order to have a world championship. They played the Saint Louis Cardinals, who had won more world championships than any club except the Yankees. The Red Sox came into the series on a four-game winning streak and amazingly won four straight to sweep the Cardinals and win their first world championship in eighty-six years. The greatest baseball comeback was now complete.

Abraham Lincoln

Many (myself included) consider Lincoln to be the greatest president in the history of the United States. He led the country through its greatest moral and military crisis, essentially saved the country from destruction, and directed it toward restoration.

Lincoln grew up in meager circumstances. His mother died when he was just nine years old; for his education, he was essentially self-taught. He tried his hand at business and failed at it not once but twice. During that time, he ran for his first elected office and lost. His first true love died probably of typhoid fever, and Lincoln had what most today would call a nervous breakdown.

Though he was elected to four terms in the Illinois House of Representatives, Lincoln lost when he ran for the US Congress. He ran twice for the US Senate and lost both times, as well as losing the election in 1856 as the vice presidential candidate. Previous to his run for the presidency, Lincoln had won only one national election in his entire political career. Although he experienced an incredible number of setbacks in both his personal and professional life, Lincoln would make one of the greatest comebacks in history.

In 1860, Lincoln was elected the sixteenth president of the United States, marking the beginning of his remarkable comeback. His presidency began with the secession of the Southern states and the beginning of the Civil War at Fort Sumter. Lincoln had the immense challenge of directing the war effort, handling his normal presidential responsibilities, and dealing with the criticism of antiwar Democrats. He showed deft political skill and leadership acumen in dealing with all of his challenges.

Lincoln had many great accomplishments that solidify his place in American history and reveal the greatness of his comeback. His speech, the Gettysburg Address, is the most quoted speech in American history. The Emancipation Proclamation freed all slaves and stands as one of the greatest acts of moral leadership in history. His reelection in 1864 confirmed that his continued leadership was vital to the country, and his approach and attitude toward the defeated Southern states helped reunite the nation.

Without Lincoln, the United States would look very different today. Considering his many setbacks, what he accomplished mark his comeback as one of the greatest of all time.

Jesus Christ's Resurrection

Jesus was the most important person who ever lived. His life, death, and resurrection literally changed the course of human history, experiencing the ultimate setback and the ultimate comeback.

Jesus began his life miraculously, having been born of a virgin. Conceived by the Holy Spirit through the Virgin Mary, Jesus was literally both God and man. Jesus was unique, which was recognized by the religious scholars of his day when he was still young.

Jesus launched his public ministry when he was thirty years old. He overcame the temptation of the Devil in the desert, proclaimed himself to be the Messiah, and gathered together a team of twelve disciples. He traveled throughout his region performing good works, healing the sick, and teaching God's message. He performed many miracles and created quite a stir amongst many religious leaders. Jesus predicted that the kingdom of God would come, but it would not be an earthly kingdom or a political revolution. Rather, Jesus would become the leader of each individual's life and establish his teachings as the way to live. Many chose to become Jesus' followers, and he gained great popularity with the general public.

Jesus lived a perfect, sinless life. However, the religious leaders of his day viewed him with suspicion and disdain and convinced one of Jesus' disciples to betray him. Jesus was then arrested and brought before the Roman authorities for punishment. Pilate the Roman governor did not think Jesus was guilty of anything but gave them a choice. They demanded that Jesus receive the death sentence.

Jesus was guilty of no crime and had done incredible good, yet he was crucified, the most painful and horrendous death in the ancient world. His hands and feet were nailed to intersecting wooden beams, which were then lifted up and placed in the ground. In order for Jesus to breathe, he had to lift himself up, tearing His flesh in the process. Every moment on the cross, Jesus was in excruciating pain and was mocked, ridiculed, and spat upon. Jesus also had a crown of thorns placed on His head and His side was pierced with a sword. Finally, Jesus died. There can be no greater setback than to be cruelly and mercilessly killed.

Jesus died on a Friday. Some women went to the cave where he was buried on Sunday morning and found the stone in the front of the tomb rolled away. Jesus was not dead but had risen from the grave! The greatest comeback in history had taken place. A dead person had come back to life; death had been beaten. Jesus then appeared to His disciples and explained to them what had happened.

Jesus died as a sinless person for all the sins of humanity, and his resurrection proved his victory over sin and death. Anyone who confesses their sins to Jesus will be forgiven and granted eternal life. Thus, because of Jesus' comeback, any person can have their greatest personal comeback. The setback of mistakes, failures, and sins can be forgiven. The comeback of inner peace, purpose, and meaning in life is now available. We can live our lives in a personal relationship with God, experience his plan for our lives, and spend eternity in heaven with him after this life is over. Thanks to Jesus, life's greatest comeback is available to you any time you choose.

AUTHOR BIO

Rick McDaniel is the founder and senior pastor of Richmond Community Church in Richmond, Virginia. The church, known for its contemporary style and innovative services, has a worldwide reach through its Internet Campus (www.highimpactchurch.tv.). Rick's inspirational messages are featured in video form on www.lightsource.com and in audio form on www.oneplace.com, as well as on Audible and Amazon.

Rick has earned three degrees, including an advanced degree from Duke University. He has traveled and spoken on six continents and has authored five previous books. Rick has been married for thirty-four years to his wife, Michelle, and they have two sons, Matt and Wes.

For More Information:

www.rickmcdaniel.com
http://twitter.com/rickmcdaniel
https://www.instagram.com/rickmcdaniel44/
https://www.facebook.com/pastorrickmcdaniel